S0-AEU-751

HAND

TO

HAND

HAND
TO
HAND
FROM COMBAT TO HEALING

NIGEL W.D. MUMFORD

CHURCH

CHURCH PUBLISHING, NEW YORK

Copyright © 2000 by Nigel W.D. Mumford

All rights reserved.

To respect confidentiality all names have been changed except in certain cases where the supplicant has asked that his or her name be used.

Library of Congress Cataloging-in-Publication Data

Mumford, Nigel
   Hand to hand : from combat to healing / Nigel Mumford.
      p. cm.
         ISBN 0-89869-348-9 (pbk.)
         1. Mumford, Nigel. 2. Healers—England—
         Biography. 3. Great Britain. Royal Marines—
         Biography. 4. Christian biography—England.
         I. Title.
         BT732.56.M85 A3 2001
         283'.092—dc21

                              2001017286

Church Publishing Incorporated
445 Fifth Avenue
New York NY 10016

http://www.churchpublishing.org

5 4 3 2 1

This book is dedicated
to my niece Georgina Sheldon
and my sister Julie Sheldon

In memory of Irene Donohoe

SPECIAL WORD OF THANKS

I extend a very big thank you to Caroline Temple, whose love and trust in the Lord shines through in everything she does, and without whose help these stories would not have been put into words. Caroline spent countless hours with me, working on the original manuscript of this book; I could not have done it without her.

Acknowledgments

There are so many to thank in putting this book together. Keith and Tom have been an enormous help and inspiration. Thank you to Dick Donohoe and his late wife, Irene, for providing a place of peace and solitude where we could quietly listen to God. Thanks also to my editor at Church Publishing, Joan Castagnone.

Thank you to my dear friends at the Wilton Rotary Club, and to St. Paul's, Woodbury, whose help and prayers got me through some tough times in the transition period of my life.

To my mentors: Avery Brook, the Rev. Canon Jim Glennon, Dr. Francis and Judith McNutt, the Rev. James Wheeler, the Rev. Carole Johansen, the Rev. Elena Barnam, the Rev. Larry Carew, the Rev. Douglas Hutchings, the Rev. Roger White, and the Rev. David and Jean Mumford and Julie Sheldon. Thank you for your teachings and insights.

Thank you God, thank you Jesus, thank you Holy Spirit, thank you Holy Trinity.

THE ORATORY OF THE LITTLE WAY

Nestled on four acres of land in a peaceful rural setting, the Oratory of the Little Way is an eight-bed retreat house with a chapel, where guests may come for an hour, a day, overnight, or longer. The Oratory is ecumenical, welcoming people from all denominations.

Retreats are available for individuals, groups, healing ministry teams, and primary care givers. Weekly public healing services are held at 10:00 A.M. on Tuesday. A public healing service is also held monthly at the New Milford Hospital.

Guests will find God's healing love and grace as they become close to God through prayer and rest.

To contact the Oratory:

P.O. Box 221
Gaylordsville, CT 06755 USA
860-354-8294
860-354-0574 (Fax)
www.cysol.com/oratory
heal2@aol.com

TABLE OF CONTENTS

PART III: HAND TO HAND

FOREWORD

I am pleased to commend to you, the reader, this powerful account of Nigel Mumford's call to ministry, and the extraordinary stories that illustrate the very real grace of God and the power of healing prayer.

The simple, yet direct narrative enables the reader to be inexplicably drawn to those people with whom Nigel has worked, and whose lives have been changed forever due to the marvelous results of prayer. *Hand to Hand: From Combat to Healing* is a deeply personal book, reflecting Nigel's own experience of transformation from Marine Commando to minister of healing. His journey began after the wonderful and extraordinary healing of his own sister, Julie Sheldon, which galvanized Nigel to become a channel of God's love and healing for others. It so inspired him that he has pursued and developed his life into the full-time ministry of healing. As is so often the case, the torch is passed from person to person, in the name of Jesus Christ. Julie is the author of *Dancer Off Her Feet*, *The Blessing of Tears*, and *One Step at a Time*.

The important message in this work is that God does, indeed, heal today. Through his grace and his devoted servants on this earth, his mighty hand is felt. It is with great pleasure and confidence that I encourage you to come alongside Nigel and be inspired by the teachings of this book so that you, too, may become a devoted servant of God.

The Rev. Canon A. James Glennon, A.M.

"When I came to you, brothers and sisters, I did not come proclaiming the mystery of God to you in lofty words or wisdom. For I decided to know nothing among you except Jesus Christ, and him crucified. And I came to you in weakness and in fear and in much trembling. My speech and my proclamation were not with plausible words of wisdom, but with a demonstration of the Spirit and of power, so that your faith might rest not on human wisdom but in the power of God."

—1 Corinthians 2:1–5

PROLOGUE

"It doesn't matter which church you go to or, for that matter, which church you stay away from, all are welcome."

—The Rev. Benjamin Priest,
Founder of the Oratory of the Little Way

It was dusk. Gentle drizzle was falling, the rain-drops mingling with the beads of sweat, which trickled down my face and neck. The stench of human excrement pervaded the air, mixed with the sour smell of smoke and spent bullets. In the distance, an occasional gunshot rang out, followed by the sound of broken glass and then, the screams.

I lay motionless on the cold, hard concrete of a narrow alley in the war-ravaged city of Belfast. My face was pressed against the unforgiving steel of my rifle, every muscle in my body tensed as my index finger tightened on the trigger. My eye never strayed from its target, the enemy.

Bile rose in my throat. Only the twitch of my index finger lay between this man's life and his death. Far from my conscious mind on that gray November day in 1972, was the thought that he, like me, was a human being, created in God's likeness.

That evening he was the hunter and I was the prey. Trapped by the gray stone walls of that narrow alleyway, all my concentration trained on my target, the seconds turned to minutes. His machine gun trained on me, my trifle trained on him. Breath held. Do I gently squeeze the trigger? He held my life in his hands as surely as I held his.

Somewhere in the distance a dog barked, breaking the tension for a split second. It was long enough. The figure slipped into the shadows and I relaxed my finger on the trigger. I rolled over in the gutter, feeling only the warmth of my own tears.

Twenty-five years later, I find myself on my knees, bathed in the peace of a chapel, cradling a sick infant in my arms. The intensity I now bring to my prayers equals the intensity I brought to that alleyway all those years before, but in my arms lies an infant instead of a rifle, and I am asking God for her to be healed. Instead of training my eyes on the enemy, I train them on the beautiful, trusting eyes of a little girl struggling for life.

God has touched my life in ways I would not have dreamed possible twenty-five, or even ten, years ago. My journey has transformed me from Royal Marine Commando to Lay Minister of Healing. Twenty-five years ago, I was trained to kill or be killed: now it is my privilege to teach people to heal and be healed.

The most extraordinary thing about my journey has been its simplicity. The gift of healing given to me to use for others, and the means by which I am able to exercise that gift, epitomize to me the simple love of God. I feel that I have "majored" in life in my heart—that place in me where the love of God resides. I have found in this simplicity that getting out of the way of God, that is to get my own baggage out of the way, to let God's simple love shine through is perhaps the message that Christ gave us two thousand years ago.

It is a real privilege to tell the stories in this book, tales of real life, of real prayers that have been answered, stories of how faith the size of a mustard seed can move mountains (Matthew 17:20). It is my hope that, through sharing these stories of miracles, faith, and, most of all, the hope that belief in God can bring, the door will be opened to those who are lost, in pain, or searching for a brighter lamp to light their way (Matthew 5:14). Whatever denomination you are (or are not), the simple gift of healing is open to you. It is my hope that these words will bring you closer to your God, and to that peace which passes all understanding.

Part I

From Combat

FROM WAR TO PEACE

"No one serving as a soldier gets involved in civilian affairs—he wants to please his commanding officer."

—2 Timothy 2:4

When I was seventeen, I enlisted in Her Majesty's Royal Marine Commandos, where I served for seven years. My time served at war is, I believe, a part of my personal journey of pain and ultimate healing which eventually brought me closer to God—but not before initially leading me further away.

In the early 1970s, I served three tours of duty in Belfast, Northern Ireland. Officially, I was part of a peacekeeping force, but in actuality, I felt I was there as cannon fodder, a human target. Fear of injury and death was never far from my mind. What would it feel like to be shot? What would it feel like to be blown up or to lose a limb in an explosion? How would I cope with the pain? I did not realize then that the worst pain I would come to feel would be caused by emotional wounds, a deep scarring that would haunt my dreams for the next twenty years.

✦ ✦ ✦

Two days before I was scheduled to begin my first tour of duty, I had two hours to "kill," while I waited for a train home for weekend leave. I had completed not only my Green Beret training, but also an intensive course in guerilla warfare for street policing. A lot of that preparation included psychological stuff, like looking at videotapes and slides of bombing victims, dismembered bodies, autopsies showing what happens in the path of a bullet. The point of the training was to render both my mind and body utterly prepared for combat. And my body *was* prepared. On the surface, I radiated Green Beret bravado. But my mind was not prepared at all. I was, in fact, terrified.

I wandered out of the train station and up a nearby hill. A steady drizzle and the gathering darkness added to my sense of despair. I walked up the hill crying, nearly overwhelmed by doubt, wondering what I had done by joining the Marines? Why had I ensured that I would go to war? Was I crazy?

When I joined the Marines, I always assumed, quite naively I realize now, that "the troubles" would be over and that I would not be involved. Now I was standing on the precipice of life, suddenly facing the very real possibility of death. My own drill instructor had been killed in an explosion shortly before this, and I was now stepping onto the brink myself. I was scared out of my mind, but much too tough to admit it. Being part Irish, part English, and part Scottish, I seriously wondered why I had volunteered to be a Marine, the toughest regiment I could have joined.

Of course there was no way out for me. Running away was not an option—my training would not permit it. As I walked up this very steep hill, the first building I came to was the YMCA. The lights were on. There was a sign saying come in.

There was apparently a youth revival meeting going on. A bunch of kids, probably aged from about ten to sixteen, milled about inside. It looked warm and they were serving refreshments. I went in…or I was led in. I don't remember making a decision; I simply walked in as if that was where I was supposed to go. It was a most peculiar feeling.

They were playing music. There was an awful din. I was obviously out of place—much taller and bigger than everyone. My hair was very short and—in those days—that made me very conspicuous. Most people knew that Marines wore their sideburns cut halfway down the ear. The people in the Navy had sideburns to the bottom of their ears, and sometimes the kids had huge sideburns, descending well below the bottom of their ears. Without being in uniform, I was in uniform. I clearly did not belong.

I marvel at what happened next. A sixteen-year-old boy, barely two years younger than me in years, but incalculably younger in experience, came up to me and tried to start a conversation. I ignored him, thinking myself much too mature and worldly wise to spend time with such a child. Finally, he said, "Do you want to meet Jesus?"

At that point, he got my attention. I looked him right in the eye and said sarcastically, "I thought they killed him two thousand years ago." I had not heard the message that Christ is alive today. I marvel at this sixteen-year-old approaching a man, a much bigger, much older marine with such a question. Then, strangely enough, I said, "Yes, I would like to meet Jesus." My words were part challenge, part embarrassed agreement. Though the Marines were in the process of "curing me" of emotion, I was still quite shy and easily embarrassed.

The kid said, "Follow me."

I did as he said, feeling like a fool. But thinking at the same time, "Hey, I could be dead this time next week. Why not? I'll take anything at this point. Whatever happens, I don't care."

We walked into a small, softly lit chapel where some of his mates were chatting in the back and in the front, jamming on their guitars. My guide boldly walked in and said, "I'd like you all to leave."

I waited outside thinking, my God, that takes some guts. Who is this kid? Everybody smiled, said, "No problem," and left. He brought me in. I felt very meek, my shoulders caved, my head bowed.

This boy, this child, sat me down. He said, "Nigel, what I'm going to do is pray. And when I finish praying—and when you're ready—I want you to open your eyes and say whatever is in your mind. I told him I didn't know the right words, the fancy words, and he assured me that that was okay.

I found myself kneeling in the front of the chapel. The boy prayed, but the only thing in my mind was "What am I doing?" Then suddenly there was silence. I bowed in prayer, half-listening to what he had been saying. I felt I had been put on the spot—trembling with fear for myself and fear of what I would say. I tried to think of something intelligent to say, but I couldn't. Then my mind went blank and a sort of peace came over me, a wonderful feeling, almost like I was washed in peace, showered in peace. It started in my head and flowed through me. I opened my eyes quite naturally, feeling no fear at all and was shocked to see the cross above the altar bathed in light. I heard myself say, "I see the light." At that moment, it didn't mean much to me. But the boy leapt up with excitement and rejoicing. He ran out of the chapel and told everyone.

I was a bit dazed, but I felt like something important had happened. The fear had gone and the extraordinary feeling of peace took its place. All the stuff that I had been taught as a kid began to make sense in a very gentle and slow way. Suddenly, Jesus had become real and my heart started to fill with joy. And I remember walking down the hill that had seemed a mountain only a short time before. It had stopped raining and I walked with a spring in my step.

I waited for my train, smiling. Everything was okay. In that strange space of time where time itself lost meaning, I was given the faith that I did not myself have. I was frightened for my life, coming to the sudden realization that I was facing head-on my own mortality. I knew intellectually that there was a good possibility that I would not come back alive; the training was over and I was left only with my tough bravado to face the cold, harsh reality of war. The missing piece was the prayer given to me by a complete stranger, a sixteen-year-old boy who understood. God is mighty.

✦ ✦ ✦

On Sunday, after my leave, I went back to camp, ready for whatever happened to me. But the sad thing was that this peace and exuberance only lasted about two weeks because there was nothing to feed the fire.

During the next four months, my life became a living hell. I was shot at three times and blown off my feet by bombs five times. I was hit in the head and blinded by my own blood in a Sunday afternoon riot that in itself was perhaps the most terrifying experience I have ever had in my life. My imagination ran wild. I did not want to raise my hand to feel what damage had been done. The pain was excruciating, the fear paralyzing.

Knowing that fighting was going on all around me, blinded, lying on the street, I dragged myself blindly back towards my commando unit. My fellow Marines did not recognize me.

Maybe if I had remembered that boy's prayer, I would have found some comfort in that hell. I did not yet understand that I had embarked on a journey that would radically transform my life.

✦ ✦ ✦

A few years later the peace I had experienced in that little chapel at the YMCA was a distant memory until a day in 1975 when my life nearly ended.

I was a young Marine, based in Malta. Like most 21-year-olds, despite the pain and carnage I had seen, I considered myself immortal, and it was in this frame of mind that I approached a diving expedition, renting scuba diving equipment with several of my friends, none of whom had any great diving experience.

It was one of those perfect summer days in the Mediterranean when the deep blue of the sea was glistening in the sunlight. It was as if the sea, the sun, and the blue sky were there for us alone, beckoning us to become a part of it. After receiving minimal instructions and doing a short test dive, we swam under water, leaving the calm, protected bay for the open sea, swimming deeper and deeper through the clear waters, following the contours of a natural underwater valley. When I reached the bottom, the silence and the peace of this completely different world soon entranced me. I sat on the sand, savoring the experience, the only sound the sigh of my breathing apparatus. I was acutely aware of the texture of the sand, the shape of the rocks, and the extraordinary underwater world I had joined. I lost any sense of time passing, until the sudden pressure in my ears shattered the magic of the moment, making me instantly aware of the depth of the water.

As I looked up to the surface, seventy-five feet away, water seeped into my mask, choking me. The mirrorlike surface of the sea looked impossibly far away. Our safety instructions had been so minimal that I had no idea how to clear my mask. I panicked. With a huge rush of adrenaline, I pushed myself off the seabed like a human rocket and, kicking furiously, torpedoing towards the surface. A little voice in my head kept reminding me to exhale, lest I get an embolism or the bends. Terrified of breathing in, I exhaled continuously for what felt like a very long journey.

Eventually, and none too soon, I broke the surface, coughing and spluttering. My mouthpiece flew out of my mouth like a cork out of a bottle. I gasped the fresh air gratefully. In desperation, and with every ounce of energy, I tried to grab the air supply and remove my weight belt, but the weights were too heavy, dragging me underwater. I summoned up my last vestiges of energy to swim to the rocky shore, clawing at the rocks, only to be knocked back into the water by the tremendous force of the next wave crashing on the rocks around me. My fingernails were splitting laterally and I was scraping away the skin on my hands with my mad, desperate clawing. Each time I got a handhold, another wave smashed against my body and pulled me back. Finally, I reached a point where I could not continue. The first time I breathed in water, I was terrified. I knew at once that I was going to die.

Then, inexplicably, my body began to relax. The water began flowing into my lungs, but there was no more fear of death, no panicked struggle, only complete calm—a remarkable peace. In that moment, I knew it would be okay to die. I was ready to let go of life. I was bathed in a brilliant beam of light, and I wanted it to consume me completely. I thought, for a moment, that I had a clear choice whether to live or die, that the choice was mine to make. I felt the fine line between life and death. I thought, in the chaos of the water, that I indeed had a choice. My mind was still capable of the fight or flight response, even though, of course, there was not much choice for me to make.

The light beckoned to me. My panic disappeared. I felt no more pain. I had no sense of my physical surroundings. I felt only complete and utter peace, a peace more profound than I had ever experienced before, an all-consuming inexplicable peace, a peace that reassured me that, whether I lived or died, all would be well.

I was wrenched back to reality when I regained consciousness and found myself in the back seat of a car, vomiting. Some Navy divers had seen my body floating, motionless, on the surface of the sea like a dead seal. They had staged a rope rescue and resuscitated me, saving my life. The sudden and complete awareness of reality overwhelmed me. I knew we were driving too fast on the wrong side of the road, heading straight for a collision with an oncoming car hurtling towards us. For the second time that day, I thought the end had come.

I spent the next three days in the hospital; the first hour a helicopter stood by to take me to a decompression chamber, should it be necessary. My body was bandaged from head to toe, promptly earning me the nickname "Mummy Mumford." During the three days I spent in the hospital, the question formed and reformed in my mind—"Why am I alive when I shouldn't be?" For years, the answer to this question eluded me. However, I was certain of one thing—I had been saved for a reason.

Twenty years later, I see this episode as a crucial signpost on my journey. I have found myself drawing on this experience on many occasions, especially with patients who are close to death, for I have personally experienced that peace that passes all understanding. Since that episode, I do not fear death. I understand it is an acceptable part of living and, for many of us, at the proper time, an inevitable part of living.

✦ ✦ ✦

It is never a simple thing to humbly seek healing. Painful memories, memories quite difficult to face, often get in the way. But God is there and understands our experience and the power it has over us.

One sunny afternoon, on a week's leave from active duty, I went into the village with my mother to do some shopping. I was edgy and nervous, finding it very hard to switch my headset from a cold, hostile war zone to this sleepy English village where everyone was cheerfully going about their business. The peace of the afternoon was pierced by a loud bang, only a car backfiring. But I acted instinctively—I threw my body on the sidewalk, rolled into the gutter and lay for a few moments with my hands in front of me as if I was holding my rifle. Some people laughed. My mother wept. I felt like an idiot, but I now look back with compassion at a young Marine that had been expertly trained to survive and had simply reacted to save his life.

As a drill instructor, I was a tough guy. It was my job to train recruits to be Marines, to ensure that each young man came out of basic training as a "lean, mean, green fighting machine" able to kill or be killed. I was good at my job, but, after seven years in the service, my career ended when four of my recruits were killed in their Land Rover with one bomb. In that moment, I knew I could no longer function as a Marine. After these four men died, I was unable to speak for a week and had a very bad stutter for six months. I was diagnosed with shell shock or battle fatigue—what is now called post-traumatic stress syndrome.

I left the service in the summer of 1978.

Over the years, I have worked and continue to work with veterans of the Vietnam War. We usually form a special bond and share an unspoken language, rooted in our similar experiences of the devastation and loss of war, fought for causes full of ambiguity and politics.

✦ ✦ ✦

I include these stories of my wartime experiences because there are many people whose lives have been ravaged and continue to be ravaged by the torment of war. Countless people suffer, feeling as if they have nowhere to turn with their pain and fear. I hope that by sharing some of the still-raw wounds of my own torment, I may encourage others to seek healing through reaching out to God. God's presence and healing grace brings a love and peace deep enough, not to erase those memories, but to help us to move forward in the sure knowledge of his love and caring. Even in war, God is present, holding us in his arms like babies and blessing us with healing grace.

A New Life

> "Do not worry, saying, 'What will we eat?'
> or 'What will we drink?' or 'What will we
> wear?' Your heavenly Father knows that
> you need all these things. But strive first
> for the kingdom of God and his righteous-
> ness, and all these things will be given to
> you as well. So do not worry about tomor-
> row, for tomorrow will bring worries of its
> own. Today's trouble is enough for today."
>
> —Matthew 6:31–34

There isn't much honest employment for a lean, mean fighting machine, but I had to figure out a way to support myself after leaving the service.

I moved to London, where I got a job as a handyman at Selfridge's, installing do-it-yourself hardware. I spent a lot of my spare time in the high-end antique shop, where my godfather worked serving lords and ladies, and supplying props to movies. There I learned the trade that would earn me a good living in the coming years—the art of picture framing.

In the traditional English way, the framer I learned from never talked to me about what he did. He was from the school that believed a student learned more by watching than by listening. And that is exactly what I did.

My new life had begun. In 1979, I married Catherine, who had been a member of the Royal Ballet with my sister Julie. In 1980, we moved to Connecticut, her home state. Eventually, I opened my own framing business and made quite a success of it, framing a variety of precious art works from children's drawings to a million-dollar Georgia O'Keefe.

It was in my shop that I experienced the first powerful call to the healing ministry.

DANCER OFF HER FEET

"Then maidens will dance and be glad, young men and old as well. I will turn their mourning into gladness; I will give them comfort and joy instead of sorrow."

—Jeremiah 31:13

Even though I am the son of an Anglican vicar and was brought up to believe in God, my childhood memories of religious experience are not particularly pleasant. I remember boring services held in the damp, musty old church of our nearby rural English village. I remember a church so cold I thought the candles on the altar were there to add to the warmth. I remember rushing out of one Easter service after eating too much candy and promptly emptying the contents of my stomach over Colonel Bastard's (pronounced BAR-STARD) grave. I remember the parish solving the mystery of the missing collection money—the culprits were found to be the vicar's terrible adopted twins. And, more fondly, I remember losing myself in the harmonic notes of my violin as an excuse for not attending church.

When my sister Julie lay dying in a hospital bed on the other side of the world, my fragile faith nearly collapsed entirely.

In 1989, my otherwise healthy, strong sister began to experience pain in her knee. She was, at the time, a dancer with London's Royal Ballet, so any injury that interfered with her dancing was crisis enough in itself. She had trained for years to make her body a finely tuned instrument of art. Each performance was, for me, a living oil painting framed by the richness of the deep velvet curtains around the stage. No one could know that in only a few short months her body would be ugly and broken, a distorted version of the lithe and supple body she had worked so hard to create.

This knee injury marked the beginning of three seemingly endless years of doctors, hospitals, tests, surgery, pain and lost hope. Soon she could hardly walk, let alone dance. Hard as it was at the time to see her in such physical and psychological pain, we had no idea that this was only the beginning of a long spiral into the depths of despair.

For six months, she underwent many tests, only to be told that her condition was hysterical; nothing could be done. "Go home to your family, there's nothing wrong," she was told time after time. At one point, the doctors forced her to rise out of the wheelchair and walk. In fact, the first time I saw her in the hospital, her head was bandaged from the fall she had taken. Her legs, those strong, dancer's legs, did not work any more. The doctors had no idea how to treat her. In a final desperate attempt to straighten her right leg, now curled into an awkward and painful position, the doctors put her under full anesthetic, straightened the leg, and put it in a cast. A few hours after surgery, the muscles in her newly straightened leg went into spasm and her leg broke the cast, returning the leg to its original, bent position. Julie passed out from the pain.

After this episode, her condition was finally diagnosed as a neurological condition known as dystonia. For the next three years, her body deteriorated as it succumbed to the disease, finally curling up in the fetal position. This beautiful ballet dancer, my sister, who had spent her career exercising such fierce control over her body now lay, helpless, waiting for the next muscle spasm to rock her body, anxiously begging for the next dose of pain medication. Eight to ten times a day her muscles would reverse their posture and she would revert from the fetal position to, as she called it, a "beetle" position where her back arched and her limbs splayed outwards. Her head would fly back with such force that doctors feared she might die from breaking her own neck.

During this time, people all around the world prayed for Julie. I prayed too, but without much conviction. As Julie's big brother, and a former Green Beret, my desire to act and my feeling of helplessness overwhelmed me. I felt I ought to be able to do something: "Please God, just let me *do* something," was my constant prayer.

Sometimes anger would creep in, destructive, blaming anger. I well knew how easily I could

close her windpipe and end her pain. I am still hor-
rified to remember how close I came to doing just
that. Even the memory of the moment I stood
there, contemplating killing my sister, leaves me
feeling cold and empty.

Only a few months before, I had put my dog to
sleep rather than allow her to linger on in constant
pain. It seemed to me that we were more compassionate to our animals than to our fellow human
beings.

But God does indeed move in mysterious
ways, and less than twenty-four hours after this terrible moment of despair the miracle of Julie's healing began. A close friend of Julie's invited Canon
Jim Glennon, an Anglican minister from Australia,
to pray with Julie. He spent half an hour with her,
praying with her in simple terms, reassuring her
that he and many others believed in her healing.
That afternoon, for the first time in months, she sat
up in bed unaided; the next day she hobbled to the
window. Though she suffered a few relapses,
Julie's body began to return to normal. She
weighed only seventy-five pounds, but the raging
battle in her muscles had quieted and she was able
to begin to rest peacefully and regain some of her
health. The miracle of her physical healing had
begun. The emotional healing would take months
longer.

She struggled to find forgiveness and dispel
her anger at everyone who had caused her so much
pain. Her addiction to the prescribed pain-killing
drugs took three more months to heal.

Julie's neurologist, a well-known London professor and England's leading authority on dystonia was quoted as saying, "This indeed is a miraculous healing." In my own life, the witness of Julie's healing not only restored my faith in God, but also strengthened it to a point of total commitment to the hope that God brings, even in the darkest hours of our lives.

Julie never danced again, but she has become a beacon of hope for many who are suffering from disease, illness, and disbelief. Today, Julie tells her story all over the world, through her books and her speaking engagements. She is healthy, pain-free, and completely healed.

STEPPING OUT OF THE BOAT

"There are different kinds of fruits, but the same Spirit. There are different kinds of service, but the same Lord. There are different kinds of working, but the same God works all of them in all men. Now to each one the manifestation of the Spirit is given for the common good. To one there is given through the Spirit the message of wisdom, to another the message of knowledge by means of the same Spirit, to another faith by the same Spirit, to another gifts of healing by that one spirit, to another miraculous powers."

—1 Corinthians 12:5–10

Following Julie's miraculous healing, my faith had been incubating, but I had no awareness or knowledge of the gifts of the Spirit, as described in 1 Corinthians.

I first experienced the manifestation of the Spirit within me on a fall day in 1990. One of the employees in my framing shop had been complaining of a headache. At the end of what had turned out to be a very busy day, I asked Betty how she was doing, barely acknowledging her answer that she was still in a great deal of pain. I turned back to what I had been doing. However, in the midst of my distraction, I astonished myself when I felt a light touch on my wrist—though no one was near me—and found my hands drawn, with no conscious effort on my part, to her head.

I think I must have given a lot of subconscious thought to prayer since Julie's healing because I did not *decide* to lay hands on Betty. I simply found myself praying silently, asking God to take the headache away. As soon as my hands touched her head, she looked at me in astonishment and said the pain had gone. I shared her amazement and felt another, equally powerful emotion—fear. I knew that in this moment my life had changed. God had taken over and I had no idea where he was about to lead me.

✦ ✦ ✦

As it happened, the next day, I left on a long-planned trip to visit my parents in England to celebrate their fortieth anniversary. With a certain amount of trepidation, I broached the subject of healing with my father. I did not know quite how to begin, so I plunged ahead, "Dad, something happened. I'm a bit worried. Can you help me?"

In the ensuing conversation that began at lunch and continued into the evening, he told me that he himself had been in the healing ministry for over twenty-five years and witnessed many miraculous healings, yet he had never told me. I imagine he thought that as a Royal Marine I would not be interested in the healing ministry. And, to be honest, at the time he was most probably right. I have never been so close to my dad. We were in such deep conversation that, before we knew it, my mother arrived with more food. Rather dismissively, we told her we had just had lunch, but she was insistent that it was seven o'clock and time for dinner.

During our talk, my father emphasized the need to "be available." Of the many stories he told me, one in particular comes to mind. Dad worked as a rural dean. Atypically, he had a day to himself with no appointments on his calendar. Though he was not required to be anywhere, he felt an overwhelming urge to get in the car and start driving, which he did, praying the whole time.

While he stopped at a crossroads, an ambulance approached. The driver was frantic, completely lost. Dad led him to the house and they arrived in time to save the man having a heart attack—one of Dad's parishioners. "Be available." I have tried to be that. It is the rock upon which I have built my ministry.

Dad wasted no time: for the first time, I was to participate at a healing service in his church the next day as part of the prayer team.

I had fallen into the deep end of the pool. Me, Nigel, at a healing service. Touching people for prayer? I simply prayed in silence.

I remember that one of the first people I touched was a man with a bad shoulder. He left the service with a big smile on his face.

Questions crowded my mind: What is happening in my life? Where am I going?

As I traveled home, I puzzled over many questions, doubts and uncertainties. But I knew that these days spent with my father had been another step in my journey to become an "employee" of God. Dad's support and instruction as he prepared me for the future was a very special and bonding moment between us.

NICHOLAS

"Then little children were brought to Jesus
for him to place his hands on them and
pray for them."

—Matthew 19:13

A few weeks after I came home from England,
by a strange coincidence (or as I now call it, a
Godincidence!), I found myself in a pulpit for the
first time, addressing about two hundred people
who had come to a weeklong seminar on healing.
I had been invited to Trinity Church in Tarriffville,
Connecticut to introduce Canon Jim Glennon from
Australia. Canon Glennon was already an important figure in my life, although we had never met
before.

I prepared an introduction based on the healing
of my sister, Julie Sheldon, and of the profound
effect her healing had on my life. Even though I
was prepared, I was very nervous. I gripped the
lectern so tightly my knuckles were white.

However, as I stood up to speak, I felt intense
heat fill my spine. I turned around to see if something behind me caught fire, but all was normal.
When I turned back towards the congregation, I

had a strange feeling of growth; my lungs filled with air and I felt physically taller. Raising my head up, I let go of the lectern, no longer holding on to it for dear life.

From that moment on, my prepared speech went by the board, and I have no idea what I said. Instead of keeping my eyes focused on the wall at the back of the church as I usually did when I spoke in public, I allowed them to roam up and down the pews looking into the eyes of every person in the church. I understand now that the heat I felt was the Holy Spirit entering me.

This was to be my much-needed second conversion, having roamed away from God for the previous twenty years. I had seen God's healing light once before, when I grasped so desperately at the rocks on my scuba-diving trip to Malta. Now I felt that light entering my very being.

A week later, I found myself at St. Barnabas Church in Ardsley, New York, again introducing Canon Glennon. The church invited me when they discovered that the tape of my introduction of Canon Glennon at Tarriffville, which they had planned to use, was faulty.

I was happy to go, feeling a little more confident this time. After the healing service, Holy Communion was offered. I found myself at the back of the church, watching a few people leave, including a woman carrying a child. A moment later, I looked up from my hymnal to see the same woman standing directly in front of me, her child snuggled into her neck. Rather surprised, I asked her if she needed help. Her reply was simple, "Will you pray for my child?"

I was astonished. I had prayed for myself in combat as a Royal Marine Commando. I had prayed for my sister when she was sick. I had prayed for Betty who worked in my shop. But I had never prayed for someone I did not know. This was the first time anyone had made a specific request to me for prayer. For what seemed like a very long time, I did not know what to do or say. Suddenly, I remembered that my sister always asked the name of the person requesting prayer, so I asked this lady the name of her son.

"Nicholas," she replied.

"What is wrong with Nicholas?" I tentatively inquired.

She told me that her son was six years old and had been born with a misconnection in his brain. "He cannot talk; he has no motor functions and cannot recognize anyone at all."

I could not see Nicholas's face and I wondered, with increasing fear, how deformed his face must be. What a terrible thought that was. I prayed for guidance: "Help, God, I do not know what to do."

Finally, I put my hand very gently on Nicholas's back. He was wearing a green down jacket; it was quite thick, just right for the fall. I barely touched his jacket, not wanting to disturb him, thinking mostly of myself. What did this child look like, I wondered?

In my mind, I prayed for Nicholas, for his healing, that God might touch and restore his brain. I also prayed for his mother and thought of the passage in the Bible about the woman who touched Jesus' robe (Matthew 9:20). Why, I wondered, had she come to me when Canon Glennon was officiating at the healing service? I continued to pray silently for Nicholas, still not wanting to disturb him. Or was it perhaps that I had never before prayed aloud and was afraid to do so now? At the end of my very simple silent prayer, I removed my hand from his back.

My touch had been so light, I knew there was no way Nicholas could have felt the movement. But when I removed my hand, Nicholas, as if in slow motion, pulled his head out of his mother's neck and turned towards me, his eyes looking directly into mine. He did not look around, he did not search, he looked right into my eyes. Hardly the deformed child I expected, Nicholas was a beautiful child with wonderful, huge eyes, who looked right into my soul.

I have never been so moved in my life. I cried. I had cried in my life, but this was the first time I had wept uncontrollable tears, sobbing. I shall never forget the look he gave me; I have seen it many times since. I have seen it many times in people close to death and sometimes in those with whom I connect in a very deep level in prayer. Here was a child who knew I had prayed for him and he let me know it. How beautiful! How extraordinary!

I was the last to receive Communion that night. Canon Glennon suggested we talk after the service. This talk was my formal introduction to the healing ministry.

I do not know where Nicholas is. The rector of the church did not know his mother. But I would love to see him again, and I do so often in my prayers. God bless you, Nicholas.

✦ ✦ ✦

This experience with Nicholas was a turning point in my life and faith. On that day, God pointed me in a very different direction. I was to give up my life as I knew it and devote myself to a calling, a life of creating hope instead of picture frames. My goal had always been to own my own business by the time I was thirty and to be a millionaire by forty. I now know I have to be careful what I pray for; not only did I own a business at twenty-nine, but I am very definitely a millionaire—not financially, as I had once hoped, but wealthy beyond the realms of anything money can buy—a spiritual millionaire!

For thirteen years I owned and ran a picture frame business, which was to become the base from which I would begin my work in the healing ministry. Indeed, during the last six years before I sold the business in 1997, it was as likely that the customer walking through the door was there for healing as for framing.

I am still moved, almost daily, by the miraculous happenings in my own life and in the lives of others who come to the Oratory of the Little Way, the healing center of which I am now the Director. I am filled with childlike wonder, awe and excitement every time someone is healed; the sheer wonder of a tangible God who moves mountains and calms the winds and the waves makes me want to jump for joy.

For nearly seven years of my service in Her Majesty's Royal Marine Commandos, I specialized in one of the toughest areas—drill instructor. This experience ultimately gave me a greater capacity to show compassion and understand the core of pain. As a drill instructor, I often stood nose to nose with a recruit, screaming in his face, ignoring his quivering bottom lip or even the trace of a tear in his eye. I had been trained to ignore such "male weakness." A Green Beret drill instructor converting young men from civilians into fighting machines may show no compassion, and indeed may feel no compassion. It is crucial that the recruit understand that his toughness really is a matter of life or death.

Now that I am involved in the healing ministry, there is a different kind of toughness needed to deal with the constant issues of pain and sickness, which are also matters of life or death. The Green Berets trained me to be tough and lacking in emotion, but now I know how much tougher one has to be to deal with the pain I see on a daily basis, much of it emotional, much of which I must let myself feel.

I recently told a friend I am in the business of restoring hope. Sometimes that hope seems out of reach, very distant, impossible to attain, and yet by reaching out to God and asking, it becomes so simple. The power of the Holy Spirit fills the room with love and energy. Perhaps that hope is only enough to get someone through another day, or perhaps it will open a door for one human being to reach out and touch the life of another. What a wonderful world it would be if every day all of us were able to hold hope in our hands and pass it on to another.

A scuba diving accident almost took my life. When I regained consciousness, I knew with complete certainty that my life had been saved for a reason, although at the time I did not know why. I do know that I have been guided and protected by my Father in heaven, as the shepherd protects and watches over every one of his sheep. It is now so clear to me that I was meant to step out of the boat in faith and pursue the healing ministry.

The understanding of why I was saved came in a number of ways—from the miraculous healing of my own sister, from the knowing look in Nicholas's eyes, and from a hundred seemingly insignificant events. However, God persisted and kept placing signs right in front of my nose until I was forced to acknowledge them.

Several years earlier, at a time when nothing could have been further from my mind, I received a vision. I would open a residential healing center in America, and today, I find myself running one of the first such centers in the country.

Each of us has our own path to chart and follow, but we are never asked to do this by ourselves. Of course, we have free will on our journey, but God is always with us as we make our choices. The Bible says that the yoke is easy and the burden is light, but the yoke is sculpted for an individual's shoulders and fits perfectly (Matthew 11:28–30). With Christ's help, we can carry any burden. I have taken this image a step further and bought a yoke in a local antique shop that, by Godincidence, fits me perfectly. I use it in sermons and talks.

Not everyone who asks for prayer is cured, but everyone is healed in some form or another. I firmly believe that something always happens when we pray for each other. It may not be in the form of immediate physical or emotional healing (although it often is), but a door is always opened. Faith is the substance of things hoped for and the evidence of things unseen. I tell people to continue in prayer and watch in faith with thanksgiving. Sometimes healing comes in a most unexpected area and not necessarily in the way we want, but prayer is always answered, if only we are aware. After all, God does the answering, not us.

✦ ✦ ✦

I hope that the sharing of the following stories of miracles, faith, and most of all the hope that belief in God can bring, will open the door for many who are lost, in pain or searching for a brighter lamp to light their way (Matthew 5:14). These are tales of real life, of real prayers that have been answered, stories of how faith the size of a mustard seed can move mountains (Matthew 17:20). I pray that these words may instill hope and belief into your soul that God does indeed heal today.

Part II

<u>To Healing</u>

LET YOURSELF BE LED BY THE POWER OF PRAYER

"Devote yourselves to prayer, being watchful and thankful."

—Colossians 4:2

I am not a healer. God is the healer. I believe that God sees us as perfect creatures and heals us because he does not want to see us suffering and in pain. Some of you reading this book are already living testimony to God's healing power; others are not. Wherever you stand on your faith journey, it is my hope and prayer that as you read this book, you will begin to experience the hope that God offers through prayer and faith.

This sometimes requires abandoning the mind set that prayer is inextricably entangled with ministers and churches. Prayer is for everyone. It does not have to be solemn and serious; it need not be confined to hushed and shadowy churches. Prayer is joyful, a moment of oneness with God. Prayer allows for mindfulness, slowing down, taking time for a "chat" with God, to talk or to listen, to ask or to receive. Prayers can be offered at any time, in any place—while driving a car, while walking in a field, or while cooking dinner. I think the power of this practice will amaze you.

When we become comfortable with simple, "chatty" prayer, we can offer up our prayers for others and ourselves. When I first experienced God's healing power, I started to pray at the same time every morning. Soon prayer became an integral part of my day, and before long I found myself praying all through the day, not stopping and dropping to my knees, of course, but integrating prayer into whatever I was doing. There is real joy to be found in approaching each day's work in a prayerful manner.

I pray for particular people when they come to mind, and often find later that there was a real need on that particular occasion. I follow "the three-time rule": when someone comes to mind three times, I call or visit to see if something is wrong. Often I find that God has communicated a friend's need.

Even when we feel completely helpless at times of illness or even death, we can pray. God hears our prayers and will be at our side and at the side of those for whom we pray. I have found that if we allow the power of the Holy Spirit to wash over us, the right words and actions will be there for us.

I remember one day receiving a phone call from the Reverend Robert Godley, an Episcopal priest, asking me to go with him to pray with one of his parishioners. I was suffering from a stomach virus but, as if I were being led, I found myself on my way. Strangely enough, by the time I arrived at the church I was feeling quite well. We were about to leave when I touched Bob's arm and suggested that we pray before we leave. I am not normally in the habit of telling ministers what to do, but things were happening in my life that I did not under·tand and I once again found myself being led. I said nothing but listened to his prayers.

After our prayers, we went on to visit Jamie, in the hospital. Jamie had cancer that had metastasized into three large bumps on her head. Her skin was yellow and her eyes were full of fear. We stood on either side of her bed in silence, our eyes closed, our hands laid on her, ready for prayer and…waiting. I wondered why Bob was taking so long to get started. After what seemed like an age, I opened one eye, in cartoon character fashion, and looked at him. To my horror, I saw that Bob was staring at me. He then asked me to lead us in prayer.

I felt the panic rising. Why was he asking me? What was I supposed to say? I silently prayed my favorite prayer, "Help me, God."

Then, to my great surprise, words poured out of my mouth, words I did not create, as I prayed for Jamie's healing. This was the first time I had ever prayed out loud. Praying aloud can be a very unnerving and huge step for most of us, a bit like stepping out of the boat and believing we can walk on the water (Matthew 14:29). What a feeling to be touched by the Holy Spirit in this way that even the words of a prayer are given to us! My hands became very hot and beads of perspiration formed on my forehead, my body twitched uncontrollably as I prayed for Jamie, a complete stranger, with words given to me by God. A long silence followed. Finally I dared to open my eyes and saw the look in Jamie's eyes, a look of peace, of connection. It was a look I had seen before, the look in Nicholas's eyes, where I had recognized the look of souls connecting in God's love and peace. Jamie's skin was now pink and normal looking. I knew beyond a doubt that the Holy Spirit had touched us.

A month later I was shocked to hear that Jamie had passed away. She had not been cured after all. That is, I would soon discover, she had not been cured physically, but there had been healing.

Over the next several months, I came to understand that in death there is an ultimate healing. After Jamie's funeral, I learned that the extreme anger felt by her husband and two small children because Jamie was leaving them had been lifted the moment we had prayed for her, allowing Jamie to die peacefully, leaving behind a family that had begun the healing process. I was beginning to learn that the greatest thing is not prayer, but answered prayer. I have also learned that we should not anticipate the answer.

Though it may feel strange and unfamiliar, let God lead you in your prayers. We need no special power, only the willingness to be open and be led to ask God to heal. This is the power of God. A small speck of faith from any one of God's creatures is enough. After all, God has assured us that: "I have heard your prayers and seen your tears; I will heal you" (2 Kings 20:5).

THE POWER OF PRAYER AND THE PRACTICE OF MEDICINE

> ...Prayers are the stairs
> That lead to the Lord,
> And to meet Him in prayer
> Is the climber's reward.
> —Helen Steiner-Rice
> "In the Vineyard of the Lord"

Over recent years, there has been a growing attempt by academics to establish a scientifically discernible link between prayer and healing. Naturally, proving this type of link in a laboratory-type setting is difficult, if not impossible, yet I find it tremendously exciting to see a growing movement within the medical profession to recognize the simple fact that, in many cases, prayer does legitimately affect the recovery of patients.

There have been a number of controlled studies done to investigate phenomena that scientists and the medical profession are beginning to recognize. Interestingly enough, research findings support prayer as an active way of introducing positive thinking into a negative situation, especially in the area of terminal illness. However, because prayer

can be, and is used in a variety of ways, it is difficult to categorize into any conclusive evidence.

A number of physicians now recognize the
power of prayer in their patients' healing. Most of
the physicians I have spoken to have prayed for a
patient at one time or another. I recently received a
letter from a surgeon who was healed of very
advanced and aggressive breast cancer through
prayer. Her story is all the more powerful for me
because she performs surgery on breast cancer
patients, many suffering from the same cancer as
her own.

The medical profession appears to be adopting
a broader attitude and recognizing methods of healing to complement the traditional drugs and
surgery. Increasingly I find myself working closely
with doctors, psychiatrists, and psychologists on a
daily basis to form a working link between my
ministry and their medical profession. And it is a
link we are forging, not a replacement—prayer
should be used with, and not in place of, traditional
medical methods.

Randolph Byrd, a cardiologist and a practicing
Christian, conducted a study designed as a scientific evaluation of the role of God in healing. Patients
in the coronary care unit of San Francisco General
Hospital in 1988 participated in the study.*

Over a period of ten months, 393 computer-
assigned patients admitted to the coronary care

---

*   Study described in Larry Dosy, M.D.'s book, *Healing
Words*. New York: Harper Mass Market Paperbacks, 1997

unit received the same medical care, with one variable—some of the patients were prayed for daily by prayer groups outside the hospital, others were not. The study was a random, double-blind experiment in which neither the doctors, staff or patients knew who was being prayed for. The prayer groups were given the first names of their patients as well as a brief description of their diagnosis and condition. They were asked to pray, but were given no specific instructions.

The results of this study showed that patients who were prayed for fared significantly better than the ones who were not prayed for. The findings of this study created a sensation and came under sharp criticism but nevertheless opened up the door to explore the power of prayer and to conduct subsequent studies, many of which have shown similar results. Surveys have been conducted which show that those who claim to feel the intimate presence of a higher power have better health and more rapid recoveries. Of course, a true believer has no need of scientific studies to prove the efficacy of prayer as he or she is able to fall back on his or her own beliefs in God. It is this peace and hope that healing can bring about so powerfully.

Many critics and non-believers say that it is misleading to say that prayer heals, since we all die in the end. However, studies have shown that the presence of a strong belief in the healing power of prayer has been found to be significant in reducing physical and/or mental stress, pain, and anxiety. But the benefit of prayer can never be scientifically proven: proponents of working prayer will always be able to outline instances when prayer works; skeptics will always be able to argue that the healing effect had nothing to do with prayer. This is where we fall back on our inherent faith as we learn to listen, love, and pray.

Interestingly, it appears that even skeptics continue to pray for one another, with an attitude that says, "What harm can it do?" It has been suggested that medical care is often inattentive to the spiritual needs of patients, that spirituality is viewed as passive rather than active. I believe this view is changing rapidly because of the increasingly positive attention the ministry is now getting. In some cases, in fact, medical students are teaming up with chaplains to observe the role of faith on patients' progress in hospitals.

I believe there is an inherent wish in all of us for hope, and specifically hope that prayer can bring. After all, confrontation with illness, death or crisis can lead us to question the very meaning of life and suffering is often the base from which a new spiritual dimension is added to our lives.

Wherever one stands on this issue, it is fascinating to note the effect that prayer has on healing from controlled studies in the medical field. It would seem that most of us are willing to try prayer as an additional alternative to medical intervention, which leads me to conclude that our spiritual core as human beings is closely interwoven with all aspects of life.

THE MANY ROOMS OF GOD'S HOUSE

"In my father's house are many rooms; if it were not so, I would have told you. I am going there to prepare a place for you."
—John 14:2

Doors open and doors close in our lives. One day, when I was just finishing my afternoon cup of tea, the door to my frame shop flew open and the room was filled with the overpowering presence of a woman declaring she had come "as a last resort." I cracked some joke about the poor quality of the other local picture framers, only to be interrupted and told quite categorically that what she wanted was healing, not framing.

Carol, and her husband Ron Galy are chiropractic doctors. Carol was raised in the Christian faith while Ron was Jewish. Two years before, she had been hit broadside by a drunk driver and had suffered a neck injury. She still suffered chronic pain from that long-ago injury. This couple's frustration, given their shared profession, was enormous, but it seemed that nothing could be done to relieve Carol's pain. She had received treatment from various sources, and she had taken pain medication, all to no avail. She remained unable to work. As is so often the case, her visit to me, in her mind at least, was indeed a "last resort."

Carol had heard about the healing gifts of God through a friend, someone who had already experienced God's healing grace first-hand. Through the simple act of asking for prayer, she was accepting the need for a broader perspective, not only for herself but also for her own patients, the need for her as a doctor to see the bigger picture.

We went to the local church where prayers were offered up both for Carol's healing and for forgiveness of the driver who had hit her. Many tears were shed before Carol left the church. Later that same day, tired and overwhelmed, she and Ron attended one of my talks. They seemed to be uncomfortable, but their presence there, together, was to have real meaning. A week later, Carol called me. She was feeling better for the first time in many months, and she and Ron were quite clearly astounded by what was happening in their lives. Her eyes were clear and there was a new energy flowing through her. But it was her husband's reaction that astonished and delighted me. As well as showing an obvious interest in the mechanics of healing prayer, he wanted to know who this Jesus was. To the best of my ability, and in very basic terms, I told him who I think Jesus to be and what he means to me. Quietly, and yet with a depth of purpose, he said, "I want Jesus in my life." With no further words needed, he dropped to his knees and Carol and I laid hands on him, asking that he might come to know the Lord. Emotions were running high, and as tears fell from his eyes, Carol and I wept with him. The mingling of our tears marked a sharing of faith, of hope, of thanks for the healing which had taken place. Ron was recently baptized.

As always, there was a ripple effect in this story. Ron offered one of the many rooms in his office (John 14:2) to me for the practice of healing prayer, and I began work there on a regular basis, praying with many of his patients suffering from chronic ailments. He extended his own healing hands to join with those of a mighty God, to better serve all those who were to come to him in pain.

PLUGGING INTO THE POWER

> "And he said to them, 'I tell you the truth, some who are standing here will not taste death before they see the Kingdom of God come with power.'"
>
> —Mark 9:1

A few weeks later, while working in Ron and Carol's chiropractic office, I counseled a man who was harboring great anger. He believed in fate and the natural order of things in life, but he had very little belief in God's part in all of this. He was a computer wizard, and we were able to identify ways in which he could dispel his anger using computer language. I suggested that he type the word "anger" on the screen, or perhaps even the causes of his anger, and slowly and deliberately dump the words into the trash, using the computer mouse.

He was able to relate to this action, using it several times successfully, and found it to be, for him, a definitive yet peaceful way of dispelling this anger. On a subsequent visit, we were able to take this concept even further by using the analogy of "plugging in" to God's power in order to make the electrical connection needed to receive healing, in the same way as a computer needs power. He was able to imagine himself "plugging in" to the Trinity: Father, Son and Holy Spirit, in the same way as we insert a plug into an electrical outlet to access power for a computer. It is not dissimilar to making the sign of the cross on ourselves as we enter church. After all, what is God's power other than a deep and direct spiritual connection between him and us?

ACCEPT YOUR HEALING

"Do you want to get well?"
"Sir," the invalid replied, "I have no one to
help me into the pool."

—John 5:7

Canon Jim Glennon talks much about accepting your healing, even as it is happening, and thanking the Lord for it in that moment. I am reminded of Kathy, a friend and customer who came into my frame shop one day, white as a ghost and doubled over in pain. She told me that she had cysts on her ovaries and had seen a doctor several times over the past few days. The probability of surgery loomed.

Kathy had read my sister's book and knew a bit about the things that were happening in my little frame shop. As she was leaving, she hesitatingly asked me if I would pray with her. Her request seemed almost an afterthought.

In cases where I do not feel it appropriate for me to lay my hands on someone's area of complaint—in this case the young woman's abdomen—I ask the supplicant put her own hand on the area of pain, while I place mine on her head.

As I did so to Kathy, I received a jolt, as if my hands had been shot through with electricity. She gave me that increasingly familiar look of knowing, as if in that moment she was accepting the gift of her healing.

Later that day, she called me. Her pain had disappeared as she left the store and she was frightened. I told her to trust in God and to thank him deeply and meaningfully. The next day she called again. During her doctor's visit that day, he could find no sign whatsoever of any cysts. Here was a medical doctor confirming this extraordinary healing experience. I was as astonished as anyone. But Jesus told us that if we ask, we shall receive, and who are we to question his word (Matthew 7:7)? I fell to my knees and thanked God with all my heart for what had happened to Kathy.

DEATH—THE ULTIMATE HEALING

> "My soul is overwhelmed with sorrow to the point of death. Stay here and keep watch with me."
>
> —Matthew 26:38

It is a pleasure to write about the joy when healing does happen, but the stories do not always have happy endings, at least on the surface. It is hard to accept and understand when the healing we ask for does not happen, even though all the "conditions" would appear to be the same. It is then that we are humbled into the understanding that our lives (and deaths) are in God's hands.

In our culture, death is a taboo subject, something we prefer to ignore, something we certainly don't want to discuss or contemplate. We tend to think of it negatively, as something completely undesirable, failing to take the time to examine its true meaning and its full implication. With this in mind I want to share some of my experiences that conclude without fairy tale "happy" endings, experiences which have forced me to look deeper in order to comprehend and accept that death is, in fact, the ultimate healing.

In July 1998, I visited the Holy Land. In the Garden of Gethsemane in Jerusalem, I read these words spoken by Jesus: "Father, I don't understand you, but I trust you." These words helped to put the healing ministry into perspective for me. Death is frightening. There is certainly a great deal of both loss and pain when a loved one dies. Death is usually hard to understand; we constantly ask, "Why?" We cannot, for example, understand how the death of a child could possibly be the will of God.

I am reminded of an occasion when I was asked to pray for a newborn whose tiny still form lay in an incubator in the intensive care unit of Bridgeport Hospital. Adrienne, a friend and colleague who joined me in prayer on this occasion was so moved by this experience that she wrote about the experience from her own perspective. I am including that story in its entirety.

> Two, three, four, five, six. The elevator rose at an alarming rate. My heart was beating fast. The doors opened at the sixth floor and we stepped tentatively out into the hospital corridor and turned towards the Pediatric ICU unit. I walked noiselessly, as if the slightest noise would allow my emotions to explode. My heart was heavy; I knew even then that this was to be a test of my faith in the power of prayer.
>
> We opened the door to the parent lounge. Two solitary figures sat silently,

hands touching, faces blank as they stared ahead, oblivious of our arrival. We approached them cautiously.

"Wendy?" I said. Her outstretched hand was cold, her pale skin like wax, her now shapeless body, swathed in dull and lifeless shades of gray. Her sunken eyes were rimmed with dark shadows from lack of sleep. The pain radiated out from her. Her elderly father sat next to her, walking stick in hand, unable to hear despite his hearing aid, his helplessness showing like an open wound.

The door opened and the baby's father and grandmother approached us, holding a tray of sandwiches. There was death in the father's face, as if he had already given up hope. I looked into his eyes, and tried to reach out to him from the bottom of my soul.

"Shall we pray together?" Nigel suggested. We all joined hands, strangers brought together by God to pray for this new life lying in an intensive care crib down the corridor. I closed my eyes, clutching the grandmother's hand in mine and sensing rather than seeing her quiet tears as her body gently shook. All heads were bowed, and through their silent cries, which came full circle through my own body, the unspoken message of hope was still alive. Silence pervaded the small, green-walled room. Two cots in the corner were cluttered with the belongings of these two parents who had held vigil for their dying daughter for six days. All I could do was send to this devastated family my hope and love as I tried to allow it to flow from every pore of my skin.

We left the grandparents holding each other, not knowing how to deal with such grief, as the four of us walked slowly down the corridor to ten-day old Adrianne. I couldn't help but note the colorful border on the walls depicting happy children, playing, jumping, laughing; all things that this baby would probably never do. But I had to believe; I was here to bring hope and pray for the miracle of life. I had to believe that this baby would one day run and shout for joy just like these other painted figures.

As we approached the little body, the nurses in their crisp white uniforms and with their kindly smiles, seemed to glide gently away. So this was Adrianne. Her mother looked lovingly and proudly from the baby back to us. She stroked the baby's skin and caressed her fingers while she told us how Adrianne had stopped breathing while at her breast six days before. Now this little figure lay shrouded in white, her tiny body surrounded by wires and tubes. Her hands and feet were swollen from blood tests. A monitor showed technical readings of each breath, beeping slowly and regularly in the background.

Adrianne's father gripped my hand. He was lost, a child himself, not knowing what to do or say. His huge hands reached out to Adrianne, rearranging her blanket, gently caressing her cheek, stroking her hair, touching her tiny feet and hands, as if absorbing the physical being of his child so he could remember it for ever.

Adrianne's mother continued to touch her, tears rolling down her face and falling onto the baby's skin like raindrops, the kind of rain that brings hope and joy to a spring day after a long winter.

A deep and spiritual peace pervaded the room like a gentle breeze and surrounded each one of us as we prayed, and in that instant, the helpless little group was bound together in light and love, strangers on this earth and yet brothers and sisters under God.

My hand hurt from the father's iron grip, but I knew that any movement from me would break the magic of this moment and the peace that surrounded us. Adrianne's little chest continued to rise and fall, her eyes flickering from time to time as her tiny fingers involuntarily tightened their grip around mine.

Adrianne died the following day when they turned off the life support. A previously undetermined genetic condition meant that she could not have lived; she was not yet ready to come to this world. I wept for that family and for that brief life. The passing of this baby deeply affected me, but even in the deep sorrow, the presence of God was profound. God bless your soul, Adrianne.

Adrianne's parents were kind enough to ask us to her funeral; in fact her mother called me no less than three times to make sure we would be there. So, on that gray February day, we made our way to the cemetery and took our seats with about forty other mourners, positioning ourselves at the back of the room. The little coffin sat on a table at the front of the room, along with some flowers and the only photo of her, taken at her birth.

At exactly one minute before eleven o'clock, her mother approached me, saying "We're ready to begin now." For a moment, I did not understand what she was saying, but then I realized that she was expecting me to officiate at this funeral. Considering my shock and the fact that I didn't have so much as a prayer book or Bible with me, I reacted reasonably quickly, and after a few deep breaths and a hasty "Help" prayer, I took my place at the lectern where I proceeded to lead a fifteen-minute service about the life of a baby I had known for less than two hours. The words just came. It was as if I was listening to the words being spoken by God into my right ear and hearing them come out of my mouth with my left ear.

Later, at the small gathering at their home, Adrianne's grandmother looked at me with such pain in her eyes and told me she would have done anything to give her life for that of her grandchild. There was no answer; there is no answer as to why death comes so unexpectedly. It is then that we have to turn to the Scriptures to be reminded that our time on this earth is finite and that we will all eventually die. Even Jesus wept at the death of his friend, Lazarus.

At times like these, I rely on a simple prayer:

> Lord, I ask that you take my tears as they silently fall down my cheek, that your healing light may shine through each and every tear to create a healing rainbow with which to surround me in your peace, love, comfort and healing grace.

In my own life, I have seen how beautiful and peaceful death can be. And, indeed, I have seen how violent it can be. I have been present at the bedside of many facing death. I have counseled those left behind, but I often sense the deep pervading peace which surrounds this harsh time for those left behind on this earth.

For example, I am reminded of the time I held the right hand of a dying man and I asked the Lord Jesus to hold his left hand. Harry was 92 and we all knew he was dying. His family gathered around us. His breathing was becoming more labored, but there was a calm air surrounding each one of us that seemed to herald his impending death. At that moment, his left hand raised in the air and then dropped. It was as if Jesus took that hand and guided his soul home, as if we had witnessed a tangible God. The peace in that room was extraordinary; there was not a sound. The words, "Be still, for the glory of the Lord is shining in this place," come to mind when I think of this moment. There was no fear, just love, pure love one for another and for God in this moment of his passing. It was this out-

pouring of love in God's name that made the dif-
ference, and I found it extremely moving when his
wife said to me, "I hope you're there when I die,"
to which I replied, "I doubt that I will be there, but
I know Christ will be holding your hand." In the
end, that is all we need to know.

After a while, Harry's wife began to weep and
there was a lot of hugging. I shall never forget the
peace in that room, even at this sad time of the
death of a loved one, as we had seen the wonder of
the power of the love of God. My first experience
of death had been in war, picking up bodies after
an explosion. As we lay the crumpled, bleeding
bodies out on the road, one of my fellow marines
found a boot with a foot in it. There were eight
bodies and one foot left over. There was no trace of
another body. In terms of my own healing, this
peaceful hospital experience was another occasion
in which death was put into a very different perspective; after all, death is the ultimate healing
experience.

Elizabeth Kubler-Ross writes powerfully of
the five stages of grieving: denial, anger, bargain-
ing, depression, and acceptance (the acronym,
DABDA). To know that we can (and indeed
should) feel these emotions in any time of loss, and
in any order, gives us permission to allow the
grieving process to take its natural course and heal
us of our sorrows. This knowledge is an extraordinary resource to have in our toolboxes for use at
times of loss, whether the loss be death, divorce,
termination of employment, the betrayal of a

friend or any other of the inevitable losses that are a part of life.

There are so many of us walking and living on this earth with the shadow of death in the form of depression. I cling to the words of Psalm 23, "Yea, though I walk through the valley of the shadow of death." We are reminded that we are always walking through the valley and we are promised, at the same time, that we will come out the other side into the sunshine.

I am fortunate—I have been shown that it's "okay" to die. We often hear tales of people on their deathbeds, hanging on to life as if waiting for permission to die. If we can learn to believe in death as the ultimate healing, then we can "let go and let God," continuing in the beauty of our lives on earth, giving ourselves permission to mourn without allowing the darkness to overcome us. Death is not darkness but light—a time to move on, a rite of passage.

With God's help, we are able to face both life on this earth and our passage to heaven.

A Heart is Healed

"The good man brings good things out of the food stored up in his heart."
—Luke 6:45

One of the responsibilities of being called to the healing ministry is to preach and teach the Word, as we are commanded to preach the kingdom and heal the sick (Matthew 10:7). My speaking engagements range from large congregations in churches to small intimate gatherings in private homes. It was in the basement of a rather large, suburban home that I found myself giving my testimony to a group of about thirty people, one of whom hobbled down the stairs on crutches, after being injured in a car accident. As usual, after my talk, people are invited to come up for individual prayer, and I usually invite the host or others to join me in the laying on of hands and healing prayer. In this instance, no sooner had the lady with the crutches received prayer than she threw the crutches to one side and literally ran up and down the stairs, much to the amusement and surprise of all of us—a true example of instantaneous healing.

The next man requesting prayer had been diagnosed with high blood pressure and expected to take medication for the condition for the rest of his life. The team laid hands on him; my own hands were on either side of his torso, one on his heart and one on his back. As I offered prayers to God, I could actually feel his racing heart slow down. This was certainly a time that I actually felt fear in the face of the awesome power of God as I sensed emotionally and physically that his heart was being healed in that very moment.

The following day, he had gone to his doctor to find his blood pressure was normal. Every day for a week, he went to his doctor, finding each time his blood pressure to be normal. He continued to visit his doctor every week, always to find the same results—normal blood pressure. His medication was discontinued.

It is important to mention here that this ministry never suggests stopping prescribed medication or interfering in any way with advice from a doctor. I often work closely with doctors and therapists; after all, we are all working to the same end in search of healing for a patient. It is extremely powerful to witness such a marriage of science and spirituality.

History and experience has shown that extremes can be dangerous in any field. In healing, it is as dangerous to disregard medicine as it is to forget that human beings are more than physiological machines. I believe that a gentle, loving, and compassionate balance benefits everyone and harms no one.

COMMUNICATION WITHOUT WORDS

"I will cry aloud to God. I will cry aloud and
he will hear me."

—Psalm 77:1

I have been surprised over my years in the healing
ministry to learn that when we give, we receive.
Jesus realized that a power had gone out from him
in the story of the woman who had been bleeding
for twelve years when he asked, "Who touched
me"(Mark 5:30). In the experience I will now
recount, I first came to realize that we are filled as
we are drained.

Several years ago I met Peter. Peter was a former airline pilot in his mid-50s, afflicted with Lou
Gehrig's disease (ALS), a terrible debilitating disease which cripples the body but not the mind.

Initially I was very uncomfortable meeting
Peter because being with him involved long
moments of silence and deep eye contact, Peter's
eyes searching my eyes for help, his gaze never for
one instant leaving mine. He was on a respirator,
unable to move or talk, his eyes his only means of

communication. He blinked once for yes, twice for no, and, with the use of a very clear alphabet chart, we were able to chat. The chart is an ingenious device that enables conversation with patients who cannot speak. Using it, a person can respond by looking at the letters of the words he wants to spell.

Overcoming the discomfort I felt in Peter's presence was difficult for me, until genuine love overcame the weakness of my fear. To see the life and meaning in Peter's eyes, his only means of communication, often became very emotional. I wept the first time we used the alphabet chart and he spelt with his eyes the letters "JES." When I asked him if he meant "Jesus," tears poured down his face.

Imagine for a moment the frustration of not being able to communicate, the agony of not being able to voice your wants and concerns. The walls surrounding Peter's bedside are covered with Bible references, sayings and meaningful words, and when you look into his eyes, you know without a shadow of a doubt that, while he may find it nearly impossible to communicate with another human being, he has no problem communicating with God. God is the only one he can talk to. The tears that are shed as we pray together, and the words, which can never be spoken between us have taught me much about overcoming my fear of silence. "Only in silence can we hear the silence speak."

For a year I visited Peter almost weekly. To be honest, at the end of a long working day I sometimes found it an effort, but time and time again I would leave feeling energized and focused. I asked him if he ever prayed for me, to which he replied with one blink of his eyes, "yes."

I was reminded that prayer often yields unexpected, unasked-for gifts. Though I went to pray for *his* healing, I found *myself* being healed of social taboos and personal inadequacies. For the first time I was able to lock eyes with a man, to look, really look into the soul of someone who wanted desperately to communicate. Eye contact is so minimal except among lovers, and I have to say I found it very embarrassing and awkward at first.

But I had found a new friend who filled me with an even deeper faith in God's love and from whom I have learned much. Peter in his silence has great wisdom in his unspoken words.

Peter has not been, and probably will never be, completely healed from his disease. However, there have been extraordinary moments of hope, including a brief period when he was able to use his fingers enough to press a small buzzer, an extraordinary accomplishment for a man suffering from ALS. But while there has not been permanent physical healing for Peter, we need to step back and consider the complete picture and see the healing that has occurred in other ways. Peter and the many strangers who have agreed to visit him have experienced the gift of prayer and friendship that has filled many lonely and isolated hours. And I know Peter gives as much as he receives. His depression has lifted. Although I and many others continue to pray for the miracle of Peter's complete cure, healing does not always come in the way we request or expect, but that does not mean failure.

OPEN OUR EYES

"O Lord, open his eyes so that he may see."

—2 Kings 6:17

Early in the days of my involvement in the healing ministry, not long after I first met Canon Jim Glennon, an artist who introduced herself as Mary, and her husband came into my shop with some work to be framed. They spent a long time carefully deliberating on their choice of frames, and were on their way out of the door when the woman hesitated, turned back to me and asked if I was still involved in the healing ministry and, if so, had I had "any luck with eyes."

"Have you had any luck with eyes?" The words resonated in my head. How did she know I was in the healing ministry? As always at such an unexpected moment, a number of thoughts raced through my mind. I was filled with empathy toward a talented artist losing her sight. I was overcome with a sense of incredulity that I had been given the opportunity to use my healing gift as God would have me do, with humility and confidence at the same time. Was it accidental that she crossed the threshold of that small frame shop that day? In fact, that very evening I was scheduled to read the news on CHRIS Radio, a radio station dedicated to providing news to the blind. What was God telling me?

I stopped by Mary's house on the way home that night to learn more about her problems with her eyes. Mary had the reverse of tunnel vision; she couldn't see what she was looking at, she could only see objects in her peripheral vision. She could not look directly at an object, but rather had to look six inches or so to either side of it. I can scarcely imagine how emotionally painful and frustrating such a condition must be for anyone, but it must cause an artist real torment. Imagine the world of an artist slowly dimming and becoming distorted, a world she had the talent to capture on canvas. Imagine her fear. Imagine her grasping as if for the last time at every image she could see, trying to file it away for the future. Up to this point, Mary had spent considerable time with numerous specialists, all of whom agreed that the prognosis was fairly grim.

That evening her husband and I sat, one on either side of her, and together laid hands on her while praying for her healing. After a half hour or so, I withdrew, leaving them alone together in prayer. When I looked back, I was moved to tears. The two of them, heads bowed in prayer, made such a beautiful image that I felt as if I had accidentally blundered into a personal, intimate moment. I could clearly see the love surrounding the couple in their belief, faith and hope.

A few days later, Mary, speaking quietly because she did not want "to break the spell," told me that her eyesight had returned to normal. Of course, I assured her that there was, of course, no "spell," only the need to offer thanks to God.

A month later, she called in a terrible state to tell me that her eyesight was again failing. Being new to this ministry and still inexperienced, I was terribly shaken by this news—why would God give back her eyesight only to take it away again? For three days I agonized, unable to shed the oppressive burden I felt. I couldn't sleep. I couldn't eat. I felt angry with God. Finally I knew that I needed to reach out.

I took my concern to the ministry-exploration training program I was undertaking at the time. There a very spiritual woman asked, with great gentleness and compassion, what I thought God had wanted Mary to see during those thirty days of restored vision.

Later, I raised this question with Mary. It turned out, she told me, that she needed to have her eyes opened—both physically and spiritually. There was an issue in her life that she needed to deal with. Though I never knew what the issue was, I do know that continued prayer enabled her to unburden herself. Once she had done this, her eyesight began to improve. Today, thanks be to God, she continues to paint, drive and function with completely normal eyesight.

WHY ARE SOME HEALED AND OTHERS CURED?

"Then the men who had been sent returned to the house and found the servant well."

—Luke 7:10

The most common question I am asked is why everyone isn't healed. My response is that while only some are cured, everyone is healed in some way. We have to understand that healing is not synonymous with physical curing. In our prayers we hope for a complete cure of the disease or disorder, but the outcome is in God's hands. Prayer is always answered in some form, but not always in the way in which we expect. I learned this lesson when I worked with Jennifer, a woman with a severe case of tennis elbow. Jennifer was seeking at best a cure, but at least some form of healing.

As Jennifer and I talked, I realized that she was having major emotional issues in the areas of guilt, loss and the impending death of her parents. Jennifer had a dreadful fear of death, despite the fact that she volunteered in a hospice. The loss of her brother eighteen years earlier had caused major problems in her life because she had not been allowed to grieve. She had not even been able to attend her own brother's funeral. Her family firmly believed in the necessity of maintaining "a stiff upper lip" at all costs. Jennifer's entire grieving process was frozen deep inside her.

She invited me to go with her back to Seattle where her brother's funeral had taken place. We went to her family's old church, and there we reenacted her brother's funeral. Afterwards we walked down to Seattle Bay where his ashes had been scattered. The immense relief and release, evident in the tears she shed, helped her come to closure. Her elbow remains painful, but doors she had never dreamt of were opened up and she embarked on a deeply spiritual journey, healing areas of her life which of which she was not even consciously aware. She no longer has any fear of death, and all guilt was lifted.

We are, of course, always seeking a complete cure for any disease. Sometimes we just need to open our eyes and see what is happening around us, rather than focusing on our very narrow idea of what we think should be happening. I was once asked to pray for a five-month-old baby, Judy. Judy had been born with a genetic disease, cystic fibrosis, and her parents were dealing with pain on many levels. They not only felt the extraordinary pain of accepting the disease afflicting their otherwise perfect little girl, but they also felt a strong sense of guilt and disappointment, even of failure, and they worried about Judy's future.

On a gray overcast day in New York City, Judy's parents, grandparents and I gathered around this small, smiley baby on the sofa. We talked about how they as parents could lay hands on her before we gathered to pray for her healing. Judy's grandfather, a physician, listened intently. All eyes were closed, except my own and Judy's, which held mine in an extraordinarily accepting bond. All of a sudden, through a crack in the closed blinds, a beam of sunlight spread its powerful rays onto Judy, surrounding her in a halo of brilliant light. Quietly, I asked the family to open their eyes. It was, to me, as if God was sending us a message of hope and love through the clouds and bleakness of that December day, that even in the shadows God is there listening to our prayers.

We seek the wonder of answered prayer; we seek a miracle, but we never know how that miracle will manifest itself. All we can do is define our request as accurately as possible and hand it over to God. Why some people are cured and some people healed, I don't know. Only God knows the answer to that one. Even Jesus prayed continually, so must we continue to pray with each other, friend to friend, spouse to spouse and stranger to stranger.

DELAYED HEALING

> "A man scatters seed on the ground. Night and day, whether he sleeps or gets up, the seed sprouts and grows, though he does not know how. All by itself the soil produces grain—first the stalk, then the head, then the full kernel in the head."
>
> —Mark 4:26–28

It is important to always remember that God heals and that we, as God's disciples, are merely channels through which he can perform his mighty work. I offer prayers for healing in faith and hope, but the outcome belongs to God. Many times I never find out how or when my prayers have been answered. I only know that they are answered—always. Sometimes healing is instantaneous; sometimes it manifests itself slowly; sometimes the supplicant is aware of "something" happening during prayer, sometimes not.

We can liken delayed healing to the parable of the mustard seed. The Gospel says that "all by itself" the soil produces grain—first the stalk, then the head and then the full corn. In the healing ministry the first step is to "plant the seed" by asking for healing prayer. We plant the seed and it germinates. We cannot see this happening until the roots begin to take hold and the smallest sprout pushes itself forcefully through the soil, seeking the light and air above. In healing, we look for such signs that the seed is taking root. Sometimes when we pray for healing the supplicant gets worse; this in my opinion is when the roots are taking hold in preparation for the advent of the stalk, the first relief. Then the stalk begins to appear, new strength. Gradually the plant ripens, ready for harvest, ready for complete healing.

This period of waiting can be extraordinarily frustrating for supplicants, their relatives, and friends. It is easy to give up and stop nurturing the seed, but it is when we cannot see what is happening with our eyes that the most important work is being done. It is easy to question the process, to want to dig up the seed and inspect the roots. But we must be patient and let them take a firm hold in the ground from which they can provide all the strength and nutrients with which to hold up the emerging stalk.

Sometimes during my talks, I am given a "word of knowledge" about some specific ailment or concern about someone in the congregation. On one occasion, this was about a woman with a problem with her right shoulder. I usually confirm it's not my imagination and rather brazenly ask the congregation directly if there is anyone with such a concern, as in this instance. A woman in the back of the church finally put up her left hand and tentatively came up to the front for prayer. The team prayed for her, and this was one of those occasions when it appeared that "nothing" whatsoever happened. For me, it is the ultimate in humility when I have stepped out of the boat with such a clear God-given identification of an injury, only to find that nothing at all seems to happen. She returned to her seat with a nonchalant shrug, feeling a little confused and forlorn, leaving me empty and humiliated. This is where, as a minister of healing, and a human being, one is reminded in a hard and humbling way that it is God who is the gardener.

The following week I was conducting the first of a four-week series on healing, to be held at a local hospital. As is often the case before speaking in public, I was feeling the butterflies in my stomach when, just to add to the stress, the order of the program was switched at the last minute and instead of speaking first, I was to be the second. I was to be launched even further out of my comfort zone when the first speaker introduced the rest of the group: seven clergy, twelve doctors, many nurses, and assorted other psychologists and psychiatrists. Feeling extremely intimidated by the caliber of the gathered community, I did not hear a single word of the first presentation, focused as I was on calming my knotted stomach and steadying my trembling hands. How, I wondered, could I speak to such a select group of professional "healers"?

At the beginning of my talk I encouraged the audience to interrupt with comments or questions. A woman put her hand up and asked, "Do you remember me?" to which I replied, "I'm afraid not." (God has given me many gifts, but a good memory is not one of them.) She reminded me that she had been at my talk the previous week and received prayer for her shoulder. She then told the assembled group of her experience the week before. To my increasing joy, she told a very happy story.

That evening at dinner, a deep pervading peace washed over her, followed by a great "click" in her shoulder, leaving her pain-free and with a complete range of motion. I knew at once that God had used this case of delayed healing in a very powerful way, not only to humble me personally, but also to lead the way for me to be able to speak to such a distinguished gathering of medical professionals about God's healing power and about how medicine and prayer can work together. I liken medicine and prayer to a set of railroad tracks, medicine being one rail and prayer the other. They run parallel toward the horizon where they seem to join together. If either one were removed, the train would not move. We can and should work together to heal.

The evening continued to build in momentum as we worked together to learn the laying on of hands in healing prayer, and at least three others then gave their testimonies as to healings they had received. I had a profound sense of the Holy Spirit flowing through everyone in the room.

Prior to this event, I had been inclined to assume that most scientists did not necessarily believe in God because of the constant application of their formulas and mathematical equations to provide answers for everything. I was wrong. Yes, there are formulas for just about everything, but one part of the formula is often left blank. That is to say, the equation is written but with parentheses which are left empty. As the Gospel says, this is what the kingdom of God is like: a man scatters seed on the ground. Night and day, whether he sleeps or gets up, the seed sprouts and grows, though he does not know how. We can add light, moisture and the warmth of the sun's rays and the seed with germinate, but we don't know how or why this happens. This is the blank in the equation that has three letters in it, and the three letters are G.O.D.!

Darwin and others had their thoughts and I suppose that I, in part, bought into their thinking— that a tested formula or a proven equation was the only way. I did not leave a place for God as I do now. The only part of a formula I can see or try to understand in this healing ministry is love.

OPEN WOUND

"Is there no balm in Gilead? Is there no physician there? Why then is there no healing for the wound of my people?"
—Jeremiah 8:22

As it does for most of us, my faith wavers from time to time, and I wonder if I am kidding myself. Sometimes, the healing ministry seems so miraculous and far-fetched that I begin to doubt that what I see and experience daily is really happening. I have such a bad memory, I need God to remind me of his awesomeness. I often find myself saying, "You want me to do *what*, Lord?" Then a glimpse of heaven is seen on earth and my faith is restored. Lord, I believe. Help my unbelief. Stories like the following one reassure me God continues to heal today.

After a service in an Episcopal church in Roxbury, Connecticut, a man called Jerry presented himself for healing prayer. He was suffering from a persistent, open wound on his left foot, which had refused to heal in over a year, and, after many visits to many doctors, the next step was amputation.

Jerry had not come to church for healing; he had not even known there was to be healing prayer that particular Sunday. He had simply allowed himself to be led there by his wife. By his set expression, I could see that he was not very interested in what we were doing and was there under duress. As we prayed, though, his face softened, filled with a look of peace.

Several days later, Jerry telephoned me to report that, in a matter of days, the wound had begun to heal. I could hear the joy in his voice as he spoke. Not only had the wound begun to heal, his doctors no longer saw any need for amputation. In addition, the depression caused by the pain and discomfort had lifted. The effect on the congregation of this Episcopal church was rather astonishing, and the ripples caused by this particular healing are still spreading far and wide.

Jerry is a strong, well-known member of the community, a "regular guy." People asked him if his healing had been real, if it really happened. Because of Jerry, many people have sought healing who might otherwise have dismissed the very possibility.

One afternoon, three weeks later, I was deep in discussion with a Congregational minister on the topic of healing. She expressed to me how difficult it is for her to believe that Jesus heals today, even if one believes, as she does, that he healed 2,000 years ago. As she spoke, Jerry drove into the driveway. More than a little excited, I leapt up, told the minister to hold that thought, freeze the frame, and not to move a muscle, and ran out to greet him. Jerry had come to give me a gift of some pictures for the Oratory, but I knew he was bringing a far greater gift, one which would strengthen faith.

At the front door, I gave Jerry a quick summary of our conversation and asked him to come in and tell his story. He beamed as he walked in proudly with no limp and proceeded to recount the miracle that he had experienced, even removing his shoe and sock to reveal the new healthy skin which had grown over the wound. The only remaining sign of trauma was some flaking skin. The three of us shed tears of joy. There were two gifts here: Jerry's healing and the gift of renewed and strengthened faith.

Despite all the wondrous things I see nowadays, the feeling of sheer joy and incredulity I feel at participation in a healing moment never fades. It wells up inside me and overwhelms my very soul with joy and gratitude.

Even Cool Kids Can be Touched by God

"To what can I compare this generation? They are like children sitting in the marketplaces and calling out to others."

—Matthew 11:16

As any parent or teacher is well aware, working with teenagers can be more than a little frustrating. Those blank stares, uninterested, far away faces, their fingers tapping out boredom, and the sense of underlying aggression can be intimidating to the best of us. It was to such a scene that I took a prepared talk to a group of about twenty adolescents at a local church, a group of 13- and 14-year-olds from a nearby private school, there at their parents insistence and quite obviously oozing negativity from every pore.

Their adult leader went ahead with the introductions despite the very apparent lack of interest from the audience. She may as well have been talking to herself, for the chatting and sniggering continued, and I realized I was going to have to ask for some serious divine intervention to help me get through to these kids. I started to pray, trying to ignore the noise, until my annoyance got the better of me, unleashing the Marine in me. In a firm, not-to-be-ignored drill instructor's voice, standing tall and upright, making direct eye contact with the ring leaders, I said, "I do not expect respect, but I do expect polite silence when I am praying. Shut up and pay attention!" I doubt that any of these kids were used to being spoken to in this manner. As they looked at me, their jaws dropped. I now had their attention.

My prepared talk went by the wayside. As an icebreaker, and to let them know that I knew they didn't want to be there, I had them close their eyes and asked them such questions as:

"Who wants to be here?"

"Who's here because their parents said they have to be?"

"Who believes in God?"

"Who believes that Jesus walked this earth 2,000 years ago?"

"Who wants to go to the Caribbean?"

The negative vibes subsided as the unexpectedly frivolous question made them laugh and feel more at ease.

I went on to talk about life in the Marines, and the boys began to pay attention. The girls were more easily captivated with stories about the healing of babies and young children. The mood in the room softened, to the obvious consternation of the class clown, a small, surly boy who continually tried to assert his position as leader by making constant disruptions.

An almost animal-like power struggle developed between the two of us, while the rest of the group was clearly unsure whether to allow themselves to be wooed by my story or distracted by his attitude. As for me, I asked the Holy Spirit for help and guidance, praying my favorite prayer, "Help!" The otherwise aggressive interactions with the class clown became lighter and almost humorous as the claim for supremacy was diminished and the Spirit began to be felt in the room.

I was teaching them about healing prayer when, in mid-sentence, I was given a word of knowledge; in other words, I was "told"—by an awareness in my own body of the site in question—that someone in the room had a bad right thumb. As I always do to make sure this awareness was not simply a product of my imagination. I put the thought aside. Only if the awareness continues to come back in that same place do I feel compelled to respond to the presence of the Holy Spirit, prompting me to ask if anyone in the room feels pain in that part of their body.

In this case, the Holy Spirit was about to move in an extraordinary way, for the bad right thumb belonged, of course, to none other than the class clown. After a pause, with wide-eyed amazement and a rather sheepish grin, he owned up to the fact that he had been in quite a bit of pain since he'd jammed his thumb catching a baseball. I asked him to come forward.

Looking more than a little apprehensive, he agreed to sit on a chair near me, and together with two girls who had shown great interest I laid hands on him, cupping his thumb in my hands. The three of us prayed for him and, except for our voices, the room was utterly silent.

After a few moments of silence that followed the prayer, this formerly cocky boy announced in sheer astonishment that he could now move his thumb painlessly. At this revelation, the group gasped audibly and the class clown beamed from ear to ear, a brilliant smile replacing his sullen scowl.

The class, awed by what they had seen, was full of questions, and we moved into the sanctuary of the church, breaking up into small groups of four, three standing and one sitting, I taught them how to pray for each other. The young person who was seated was asked, "What would you like prayer for?" Then hands were laid on him or her and silent or spoken prayer was offered. I taught them how to begin to listen, love, and pray for their classmates.

The church was filled with love and compassion as these once-cocky teenagers connected with one other and God. Their adult leader came up to me with tears in her eyes; she said she had never seen this group show such genuine empathy and caring one for another. Six previous speakers, she told me sheepishly, had given up in disgust and left halfway through their talks. Everyone had given up on these kids, except of course God, who had sent the Holy Spirit to move freely among them to open their hearts to love one another.

That evening we parted with hugs all around. These kids arrived not wanting any part of church, God or prayer, and left having been touched in such a way that they will, very likely, be able to draw on this experience at some point in their lives. Ironically, I think how even now, being in such a quiet, non-aggressive profession, it is useful to be able to call upon my Marine training.

HEALING THE ANIMALS

"God made the wild animals of the earth of every kind, and the cattle of every kind, and everything that creeps upon the ground of every kind. And God saw that it was good."

—Genesis 1:25

Some of my favorite stories involve animals. After all, if animals can be healed through prayer, how much more should we believe in God's healing grace, for they bring nothing but innocence and trust to the situation. Such was the case with my golden retriever, Lucy, who was diagnosed by my local vet with hip dysplasia, the only answer being surgery. However, after some reflection, I said to myself that if prayer worked with people, why not with Lucy. So I gently laid hands on her hips and prayed. She remained completely still while I prayed with her. Lucy seemed to understand that I was trying to help her. A few days later, she seemed much better; I took her back to the vet for X-rays and, to our mutual astonishment, there was no sign of damage to her hips and legs. He wondered, more than half-jokingly, if I had brought in a different dog. Lucy has been running around, pain free, ever since.

Sometime later, a guest came to visit the Oratory, even though she admitted to being more than a little skeptical about the whole idea of healing through prayer. Even after a lengthy session, we didn't seem to be getting anywhere. I sensed her resistance but I was powerless to do anything more than I was already doing—simply praying. Suddenly I remembered that she had a lame "puppy." In my desperation to form some sort of connection with her, I asked if she would like me to pray with her dog. To my surprise, she agreed.

As we walked to the car, she told me that the dog had a real dislike of strangers, did not like being touched, and bared his teeth to anyone who went near the source of his pain. Imagine my dismay to find that this "puppy" was a large, rather fierce-looking German shepherd, barking savagely at me through the car window.

It took every ounce of my Marine discipline to make myself open the car door. When I did, I found that the dog was only able to get out with the aid of a step stool because of the obvious pain in his right hip. I must admit I was extremely uncomfortable having this large German shepherd loose in my yard, but I squatted down to be on eye level with him. I was astonished when he came up to me, licked my face, and promptly presented me with his hindquarters. I placed my hands on his rump and prayed while the dog remained completely motionless. When I finished, he looked at me knowingly before jumping into the back of the car, bypassing the step stool without a glance.

The story did not end there, however; the dog was not only completely healed, but his mistress turned to me and said, "I'm ready. You can pray for me now." The next day, she called, ecstatic: her dog's hip was healed and her own condition was vastly improved as witnessed by her doctor, who immediately reduced her medication by two-thirds. That dog knew, even though his owner didn't, that he had come to the Oratory for healing.

I once went to visit a woman who was about to have an operation on her knee. She had asked for prayer for the upcoming surgery, and, as you can imagine by now, this was not an unusual request. However, what made this home visit wonderful and special was her puppy, who seemed to know what was going on.

The little black Labrador was extremely hyper, running around in circles, wanting to go in and out, all in all being a major distraction while we were trying to talk. There came a point where I asked her to put her leg on the coffee table in preparation for the laying on of hands. The puppy immediately came over, sniffed my hands, and went into the corner where his blanket was, curled up, and went to sleep. We looked at each other in utter astonishment. It seemed that the puppy knew what we were doing and that it was time to be quiet.

Sometimes there is unexpected and unrequested evidence of God's grace. I am reminded of a man whose life was changed in a few short minutes when faith's door was opened up to him. One of the "side effects" of his rebirth was confirmation from a surprising source.

As Michael writes: "This morning, as I was talking to my landlady, one of her two dogs came into the kitchen. Leo is a wire-haired terrier who barks at everyone, particularly men—because apparently he was abused by one before my land-lady got him. Leo is eleven and too old to change. Leo has barked at me almost continuously for the six months I've been living there. If I turn to look at him, he runs away and barks even louder. If I offer him a treat, I either have to set it down in front of him or wait for a very long time while, head turned away from me, Leo decides to take it. Only once before has he ever let me pet him, and he then drew away, frightened and barking.

"On this occasion, Leo pulled up in front of me, sat down, brushed me with his paw and begged to be petted. Reluctantly, I bent down and petted him, expecting him to run away. He did not. I even petted him with both hands. He still stayed. I stopped petting him. He brushed me and begged to be petted again."

This is yet another case where an animal's intu-ition was strong enough to sense and respond to a spiritual awakening. Not only had Michael's eyes been opened, but this small and poignant incident provided still more confirmation of God's healing grace.

I find people are very moved by stories about animals. After all, even the skeptics amongst us must admit that a dog cannot possibly be making it up or imagining it. They know when they are being prayed for, and very often their healing is instantaneous. Their innocence and trust is complete.

BROKEN BONES

"The hand of the Lord was upon me, and
he brought me out by the spirit of the Lord
and set me in the middle of a valley; it
was full of bones."

—Ezekiel 37:1

I have never become accustomed to the miracles I
see no matter how often I see them. However, I
think the most breathtaking moments of healing
are those documented by "before-and-after" pictures. Such was the case with Angela.

Angela fell down the stairs in her home and
broke six bones in both her wrist and finger. She
was treated in the hospital where her arm was X-
rayed and set in a cast. Four days later, because the
cast was causing so much pain and discomfort, her
injury was X-rayed for a second time before being
reset in a new cast.

Every week, at the Oratory of the Little Way,
there is a healing service to which everyone is welcome. Angela attended this service the day after
her arm had been recast, seeking and receiving
healing prayer for her broken bones.

After we prayed, Angela reported feeling a lot of heat and activity in her arm for the rest of the day; in fact, the feeling was so powerful she returned to her physician the following day and asked him to X-ray her injury once more. This third X-ray showed no trace of any broken bones. Needless to say, the physician could not believe what he was seeing; the X-rays were compared, and he was left with a lot of questions as to what exactly had happened during this two-day period.

Angela had her cast removed, leaving her wrist and finger pain-free and fully functional. She came back to see me and tell me of this miracle. Frankly, I did not believe her. I had seen her only the day before, still in a cast, and I questioned the validity of her claim. I remember thinking I would like to see her X-rays for myself. I think God puts a bit of Doubting Thomas in all of us for a reason.

But my prayer was answered immediately when she offered them to me, indicating that her physician very much wanted to talk to me. My faith in the power of healing prayer, and indeed the evidence showing her arm to be completely normal, assured me that such healings do indeed happen, even pure reason and logic told me that broken bones don't mend themselves in a day. Despite the evidence before my eyes, I was still full of doubt and I did the only thing I know to do—I prayed: "Lord, I believe. Help my unbelief."

The following week at the next healing service, Angela stood up and joyfully shared her testimony of this remarkable healing, X-rays in hand. The gathered congregation was deeply moved and erupted into spontaneous applause, showing their joy in Angela's healing and in God's never-ending work in the world.

THE RIPPLE EFFECT

"And if anyone gives even a cup of cold water to one of these little ones because he is my disciple, I tell you the truth, he will certainly not lose his reward."

—Matthew 10:42

Dear Nigel:

Thank you for the prayer you said for me the night of the Christmas party that made my stomach feel better. I didn't know that someone could pray for just fifteen minutes, and care so much in that little time to make a terrible stomach ache like I had go away. All you did was put your hand on my head for seven minutes and prayed, then did the same with the other hand. Thank you so much again.

> From,
> Elena

This letter was written to me by ten-year-old Elena shortly after she was healed of a chronic stomach pain at her mother's Christmas party. The scene looked like something straight out of "A Christmas Carol." An enormous tree was bedecked with all its finery; the stockings hung by the fireplace; the bright red hues of the poinsettias contrasted with green garlands draped elegantly around the house. In the background the joyful sounds of a choir could be heard singing carols. Couples chatted happily, the clink of champagne glasses adding to the music of the scene, while waiters served sumptuous and appetizing hors d'oeuvres on silver trays.

Upstairs, however, was a contrasting picture. The daughter of the hostess was lying on her bed, not excitedly awaiting Santa's visit as one would expect, but doubled up in pain, her small hands clutching her stomach. Her mother, clearly worried about her daughter, took me aside and asked me to pray with her while she tried to determine whether Elena needed to go to the hospital. I said, "Of course," and she led me to Elena's room.

I sat beside Elena and asked her permission to put my hands on her forehead. After she nodded, I prayed very briefly and simply, then I gently took my hands away. Her eyes opened wide, "What did you do?" she asked.

"It wasn't me, it was God," I told her.

She described, as only a child can do, how the pain had traveled up her spine, through her head, and had literally been drawn out of her body as I pulled my hand away from her forehead.

A few minutes later, I descended the grand stairway to rejoin the party. Our hostess, looking a great deal more relaxed, returned to her guests. She told the gathered group what had happened upstairs, and then suggested that I pray for her step-daughter who stood nearby, listening avidly.

I have to say that I was rather embarrassed to find myself quite unexpectedly the center of attention. But I soon realized that God was at work. The young woman next to me was pale and drawn; she was facing imminent surgery for an enlarged kidney stone. In a low voice, she told me how afraid she was to have surgery and how nervous she was about missing work.

The group seemed to melt away suddenly and silently, and we found ourselves alone in the lavishly decorated foyer, praying quietly amidst the balsam wreaths and twinkling lights.

I laid my hands on the small of her back, and prayed silently. I opened my eyes to find her dissolved in tears, almost melting into the floor.

The following week, on the day she had been scheduled for surgery, she called me. An ultrasound test had shown that the stone was significantly reduced in size, so much so that there was no longer any need for invasive surgery; the stone passed naturally with relative ease. She returned to work the following day, elated, free of the burdens of fear and pain.

I find that there is often a powerful ripple effect—when one person is healed, God makes his divine presence felt nearby, at the most unlikely of times and in the most unlikely of places.

EMOTIONAL PAIN TRAPPED IN A BODY

> "Day and night they prowl about on its walls; malice and abuse are within it."
>
> —Psalm 55:10

Needless to say, many of us bear psychological wounds and scars that need healing just as much as a broken arm. And often, these kinds of wounds are manifest in mysterious, intractable physical ailments. God knows our wounded places, where we need to be healed. I was powerfully reminded of this in quite an unexpected way.

Eric arrived at my frame shop one day; he was in his early fifties and had a pronounced limp. Of course, I asked him what was wrong with his leg. He told me that he was not sure. All he knew was that he was in pain. We went together to a local church where we slowly made our way down the aisle to one of the front pews.

As so often happens in this ministry, something utterly unexpected occurred. To my complete astonishment, I heard myself asking this grown man if he had been abused, possibly sexually abused. Though this may have been a highly inappropriate question and certainly not one which I had any right or basis on which to ask, I did not think about the question; it just came to me. Eric brightened with amazement; yes, he said hesitatingly, he had been abused at the age of eight or nine by his grandfather. Even more amazingly, he had kept this secret locked in his memory through two marriages, never disclosing it to a living soul until this day. Moments later, he fell to the floor, curled up in the fetal position and wept uncontrollably for a full forty-five minutes, his body racked with sobs.

When he recovered his composure, we talked about his anger and about the need for forgiveness in order for healing to begin. I asked him to visualize his deceased grandfather walking down the aisle, following with his eyes the old man's path down the aisle until he reached the altar where he would kneel, Eric at his side, offering him forgiveness. His words moved me deeply as he spoke from his heart, forgiving him for all those years of pain, for all the anguish and pain he had caused him.

Abruptly, Eric put up his hand and motioned me to be silent, saying he could actually feel himself being healed at that moment. I watched him stand and walk limp-free up the aisle. I understood at once that this was a case where the emotional pain had been carried physically in his right hip, an area close to the site of the abuse. He had suffered his torment silently for many years, but once he

was able to tell his terrible secret, he experienced
an overwhelming emotional release from his pain.
The genuine smile and look of peace on Eric's
face, together with the fact that he was so longer
limping, gave us both a glimpse of God working in
the world today.

GOD'S SYMPHONY OF HEALING

> "Hear this, you kings! Listen, you rulers! I
> will sing to the Lord, I will sing; I will make
> music to the Lord, the God of Israel."
> —Judges 5:3

In the years since I have been at the Oratory of
the Little Way, God has been moving quietly
and powerfully to allow healing to happen. The
weekly healing service, at first attended by only a
few people, is attended by an average of forty or
fifty, more than our small chapel can accommo-
date. Now we hold the service at the local
Methodist church.

People from far and wide come to this small
Connecticut town to learn, listen, and join together
in prayer.

Recently, Jim, a man with multiple sclerosis,
came to the service with his minister. He came
straight from his doctor's office; his condition was
so advanced that his legs had simply given out
from under him. This collapse just before the healing service had rendered him almost incapable of
walking. He did not request prayer, but sat in the
back of the church.

I invited him to come forward. Jim was hesitant at first, but putting a look that said, "What do I have to lose?" on his face, he shrugged his shoulders and came to me. The prayer team laid hands on him and prayed over him, as they did for many others that day. Interestingly enough, the clergyman who accompanied Jim was also somewhat skeptical about the ministry of the Oratory. In fact, he had come to a service three weeks before to "check it out." The door was to be opened wide that day, not only to Jim in his pain, but also to a member of the clergy who found himself doubting.

Later that day, I had a phone call from this clergyman. He recounted how he had called Jim's house a few hours after the service. His son answered the phone, telling him that his father and mother were out for a walk. A walk! Not only that, the son continued, but his parents were holding hands! Parents who had not been close enough to show each other any physical affection for many years.

When I spoke to Jim later that evening, it was a full minute before he could compose himself enough to speak of the healing, both physical and emotional, which had occurred that morning.

I am constantly reminded that Jesus, who walked this earth and taught the blind to see and the lame to walk, remains in our midst, casting his healing grace over all who request it. Each week, we invite the congregation to give testimony as to how God is working in their lives, and each week there are many people who joyously share stories of love and healing—stories of physical and emotional healings. Whatever the story, people who experience healing report an unequivocal feeling of oneness with God.

One week, a grandmother leapt out of her seat before I had even finished inviting testimonies. Her joy was apparent as she began to tell of the complete healing of her five-week-old grandson whom she had brought for prayer the week before. The little boy had a strangulated hernia and twisted intestine and was scheduled for surgery the following day. In fact, they were actually on the way to the hospital when, at the grandmother's urging, they had brought the baby in to the service for prayer. According to the prayer team, the heat surrounding the baby was intense; he continued on his way to the hospital wrapped in love and hope. Upon examination, the day before his scheduled surgery, the doctors could find only the empty sac where the hernia had been and an intestine that showed no signs of being twisted and blocked. This baby with a possibly life-threatening condition no longer required surgery. In my mind, there can be no greater testimony than this.

From time to time, news of the hope that is spread reaches me later, and from an unexpected source. I am currently working with a woman with cancer. Her daughter recently had a flat tire while on an out-of-town trip. A good Samaritan, a young man, named Tom, stopped to help her with the tire and they chatted. As their conversation progressed, they began discussing the cancer, at which point

the young man reported that his dog had been completely healed of cancer through prayer at a place
called the Oratory of the Little Way. This simple
sharing of a story led her mother to become a supplicant at the Oratory. A simple message of hope,
delivered in the simplest possible way, led this
woman to a faith community that gives her love
and support and prayers for healing.

LEARNING TO LIVE IN
THE MOMENT

"We did not give in to them for a moment,
so that the truth of the gospel might
remain with you."

—Galatians 2:5

In my experience as a lay minister of healing working with those who have concerns in illness in mind, body or soul, I have found it necessary to be totally "in the moment" with the supplicant, to be right there, to be attentive. I strive to "join up" with a person, listening to what is said, to what is not said, and to what God is saying.

It is not unlike a surgeon wielding a scalpel. I feel that allowing my mind to wander can be as critical to my "patient's" health as the lapse of an inattentive surgeon. Attentiveness is a form of discipline and concentration that can shape one's entire life. Being in the moment with Christ immeasurably enriches my days.

This was not an easy lesson for me to learn. As I made the transition from operating a retail store where success depends on planning for the future, to working in the healing ministry with people for whom the future can look fairly bleak, I came to understand the importance of living in the moment—it is all we *know* we have whether we are the picture of health or suffering terminal illness.

One afternoon, after six months at the Oratory I thought, while sipping a cup of tea and staring out of a window at a deer, about the fact that I had spent most of the previous thirteen years in business planning for holidays that were months away—Christmas, Valentine's Day, Mother's Day, Father's Day, Secretaries' Day, and so on. I realized that I needed to let go of the habit of looking to the future. I no longer needed to do that because all of time is in God's hands, and I have come to believe that planning is infinitely less important, less desirable than savoring each moment. Living at the Oratory, it is, perhaps, easier for me to practice awareness, but I also think it is a habit everyone would do well to cultivate.

Certainly, I continue to plan. Who among us could survive without it? Indeed, prayer could be considered planning for the visit of a supplicant. I also have to plan ahead for conferences, homilies, speeches, talks, missions, and the like, but those things are no longer goals to be attained or missed, they are part of a lifelong process.

✦ ✦ ✦

There are many moments in which we want nothing so much as for it to be over. It is easy to think of places where we don't want to be. Perhaps you are sick and in pain. Perhaps you are sitting in a jail cell. Perhaps you have just lost a loved one. Or perhaps this is a painful time and all you want is to get out of this moment right now, to leave the pain behind and get on with things.

And, let's face it, we all go through those terrible places of darkness. How can we deal with them? How is it possible to stay focused?

These days, the first thing that comes to my mind is that this is a time to be surrounded by a powerful prayer team. During difficult times, we cannot let ourselves be too proud to lean on those who are praying for us. To realize that others are praying and that we can let them carry us in that prayer is a wonderful comfort. Gather their prayers in your mind as you live in the moment. But if the pain is overwhelming, if this moment is unbearable, let others carry the burden. Hand your pain over to your prayer team and to God. Look at the foot of the cross. Look at the wood, the rock, the blood, the sweat, and the tears. Look at the dice and the robe the soldiers gambled for. Look there, let yourself know how Christ suffered and how he gloriously overcame that suffering. Leave, as Christ did, your pain at Golgotha.

Reading the Bible can anchor us in the moment. A person in despair might find kinship in the words of Job, "I despise my life; I would not live forever. Let me alone; my days have no meaning. What is man that you make so much of him, that you give him so much attention, that you examine him every morning and test him every moment? Will you never look away from me, or let me alone even for an instant" (7:16)? We hear Job's suffering, but look what he is saying, even in his utter despair he admits that God is with him every moment, he is not alone, though he may wish he were.

Job even goes on to say, "Turn away from me so I can have a moment's joy" (10:20), such is his utter despair. How many of us have had those thoughts? Is there anyone reading this book who has never, at some point in life, related to Job's despair?

"After Job had prayed for his friends, the Lord made him prosperous again and gave him twice as much as he had before" (42:10). Look at what happened; look at the promises in the Bible. He came through the valley of the shadow of death with twice as much. That was a glorious moment. Let us focus on the positive sign of the cross and not the "flat line" of the negative symbol. Hear the words of Psalm 30:5, "For God's anger lasts only a moment, but God's favor lasts a lifetime; weeping may remain for a night, but rejoicing comes in the morning."

The message of hope in Job 42 the "rejoicing in the morning" is, to me, like a fragile toehold on the side of a mountain—a promise that dark days will not last forever. There are many such moments in our lives, and when we focus on one moment at a time, I believe life is better

The awesome moment of the heavens opening at Jesus' Baptism is described in the wonderful words of Matthew 3:16, "As soon as Jesus was baptized, he went up out of the water. At that moment heaven was opened, and he saw the Spirit of God descending like a dove and lighting on him." What a wonderful moment. A moment I can see in my mind's eye. It holds out the promise of being filled with that love. How we need to be validated in our lives. That validation for Christ followed with the words "And a voice from heaven said, 'This is my Son, whom I love; with Him I am well pleased.'"

The Bible is filled with moments of healing. Look at what happened in single moment in Matthew 9:22, "Jesus turned and saw her. 'Take heart, daughter,' he said, 'your faith has healed you.' And the woman was healed from that moment." Paul's conversion happened in a moment. "He stood beside me and said, 'Brother Saul, receive your sight!' And at that very moment I was able to see him" (Acts 22:13).

"That moment," a glimpse of heaven, of truth, that moment of the "Ah-ha!" In a moment we can get what we are trying to learn; that moment, a tiny portion of time, a time of excellence, of importance, can, in prayer, be extended with practice.

✦ ✦ ✦

Of course we need to plan lots of things, from daily appointments to retirement and so on, but that is planning, not living. We may have a fear of the future, but God gave us a Spirit of power, love and a sound mind (2 Timothy 1:7) to overcome that fear. The past is gone; it is over. We may still have guilt, but with God's help we can let go of the pain. Through prayer, healing of memories is possible. It is not necessary or possible to completely eradicate the pain from our minds, but it is possible to put it in a place where it can no longer hurt us. We can, with God's help, rid ourselves of the tightness in our throats, the welling up of nausea in our stomach, the anxiety of a situation, by dwelling on God's love in that moment. Probably the hardest thing we have to do is to learn to trust completely in God, to trust that our lives are part of a divine plan.

Trust is a vital part of learning to live in the moment. I realized the importance of trust during a visit to the Garden of Gethsemane. In the garden is a plaque that reads, in a paraphrase of Christ's words, "Father I don't understand you, but I trust you." The simplicity and the profundity of that statement stunned me. If Christ can say, God, I don't understand you, where does that leave me in my quest to understand and plan the future? And when Christ goes on to say, "but I trust you," I knew that God can be the only place to rest. In that moment of realization I found the courage to trust, to hand it all over.

I felt, when I read that plaque, that the meaning of life became clear to me. My prayer that day was simple, "Lord God, I have not got a clue what you are up to, but let me be an instrument of your peace so that I can fully trust you and believe."

Each of us has to find our own path to that place of trust. Alice, a friend of mine, who was filled with pain, doubt, and fear from a recent divorce, told me of her way of dispelling negative thoughts. To seek a moment with God, she takes herself off alone to a quiet place of beauty where she is able to sit and talk to God aloud. For her, this place of beauty is near water, but each of us has our own haven—the forest, a quiet corner of a park, a safe and cozy room are only a few of a myriad of possibilities. Alice finds talking aloud, verbalizing her concerns, causes an immediate release because once they are out and named, they no longer belong to her alone. She can share her words and thoughts with God, perhaps at a time when she finds it hard to do so with another human being. Such is the wonder and beauty of prayer.

Alice tells me that she goes to a favorite spot on the bend of a river near her home. She focuses on the scene around her—the infinite variety of colors, the shapes of trees, clouds, and rocks, the ripples on the water, and the feeling of the wind on her face. Cupping her hands together, she blows deeply into them, physically releasing all thoughts of fear and trouble into an imaginary bubble. Then she holds her hands outwards and upwards, opening them to let the bubble float away, and then she watches as it bobs downstream until it becomes a mere speck on the horizon. Just before the bubble disappears from view, it bursts and she envisions the thoughts exploding and scattering in the air.

Prayer will help you find the best way to give up your pain. Ask God to help with your pain, your anger, with all the "emotional noise" that keeps you from finding peace. Your prayers may not be completely answered for some time, maybe not for a long time, but the simple act of saying the prayer is the first step on the long road to letting go.

AWAKENING OUR FAITH

"Why are you so afraid? Do you still have
no faith?"

—Mark 4:40

We all experience times in our lives when our faith is tested. We have a hard time believing that Jesus Christ heals today, or we doubt Christ's presence as we progress on this journey we call life, feeling alone from time to time. If we remember that even the disciples had their faith tested, we can learn from our times of doubt and take an even larger leap of faith as a result.

Many years ago, I was on board a fifty-five foot yacht in a storm in the North Sea off the east coast of England. The boat, which had no more than a handkerchief for a sail, bobbed around like a cork. Everyone was sick, including the skipper. Each time the bow disappeared into the trough of the waves I wondered if it would sink. Minutes seemed like hours as she struggled once again to heave herself up to the surface. Adding to the tension in the poor visibility was the presence of uncharted oil rigs which would suddenly and silently loom up in front of us like a city on legs, necessitating a sudden and swift change of course.

I feared that I would not survive. Indeed, had I not been wearing a harness, I would have doubtless slipped overboard, lost at sea. However, God had other plans, and after 24 hours, the storm calmed.

But immediately, we faced another challenge—all our efforts had been focused on saving ourselves and the boat; we had paid no attention to our physical location. This was before the days of global positioning satellites and we were now lost in the North Sea, only able to find our position from radio frequencies. It was terrifying and it taught me what the disciples must have felt in similar circumstances.

In Mark's gospel (4:35–41), we read of the time Jesus calmed the storm. One evening, on what appeared to be a whim, Jesus said, "Let us go across to the other side." I believe he knew what was about to happen. "A great windstorm arose and the waves beat the boat." This lake of Galilee is notorious for its sudden storms.

The gospel teaches us that Jesus was asleep on a cushion. But I believe that Jesus was, in fact, pretending to be asleep. He was lying there with one eye open—waiting, waiting for the disciples to come to him, waiting for them to say, "Help!" And I wonder if that is the case in all the storms of our lives. He is waiting for us to come to him, as surely as he is watching over us.

In their extreme fear the disciples awoke him, saying, "Teacher, do you not care that we are perishing?"

I can imagine him getting up, shrugging his shoulders and raising his eyebrows, maybe even rolling his eyes because of their lack of faith. But he calmed the storm.

I call upon this story often in the healing ministry. In sickness, we may feel as helpless as the disciples felt stranded on that lake. "Where are you Jesus?" the patient cries out in the night. As with the woman who reached out to touch Christ's robe, when we, in our sickness or stress reach out to Jesus, we are, in fact, awakening the faith within us. Perhaps we need reminding from time to time that we can reach out to Jesus when we are in need of healing. Christ commands, "Peace, be still," and there is calm. When we turn to him in our storms of stress, there will be perfect calm. When we hand over our concerns to God, our shoulders drop in acceptance and knowledge, feeling the abating waves. Once you know God is there, fearless peace enters your heart. To voyage with Jesus is to voyage in peace, even in a storm.

I also remember this gospel story in my own meditations and prayers during times of stress. I imagine I am standing in a boat watching the waves on the Sea of Galilee. Slowly, very slowly, the waves diminish, shrinking from white-capped fury to a few harmless ripples, to a millpond mirror. I look over the side of the boat and see my reflection. Standing beside me is the reflection of a smiling, bearded man, Jesus himself. All is calm and utter peace, the peace of the Lord which passes all understanding.

My prayer is a simple one:

Lord, I ask that you calm the storms of life,
that the waves of sorrow, life's problems
and anxieties, be calmed and flattened.
I ask that you remove our fears,
that those fears be removed quietly and gently
so your peace may fill our hearts,
minds, bodies and souls.
Help us to physically reach out to you
so that our doubts may be dispelled
and our faith awakened.
Amen.

PART III

__HAND TO HAND__

Practical Guidelines on Prayer and Laying on of Hands

> "Is any one among you sick? Let him call for the elders of the church. Let them pray over him, anointing him with oil in the name of the Lord. The prayer of faith will save the sick and the Lord will raise him up. And if he has committed sins, he will be forgiven. Confess your trespasses to one another, and pray for one another, that you may be healed. The effective, fervent prayer of a righteous man avails much."
>
> —James 5:14–16

The above reading from James offers, in my opinion, the biblical root of the healing ministry. In becoming acquainted with this ministry, these words need to be read and re-read to know that this is where the journey of healing begins. It incorporates the laying on of hands and the forgiveness of sins, as well as the commitment of the individual to seek not prayer but the wonder of answered prayer.

In this section, I would like to focus on the words: "pray for one another that you may be healed," and how to go about this. I will offer guidelines on how to put into practice some of the concepts of healing prayer I have been discussing. All of us can use healing prayer successfully as a form of ministry in our daily lives. As you learn more about the practical application of prayer, I would ask you to simply listen, love, and pray. Pray with the expectation that mountains will be moved, keeping focused on the resolution that will come, letting go of the negativity that undermines faith.

There is a certain amount of healthy skepticism toward the healing ministry. I am accustomed to the raised eyebrow and the comment, spoken or unspoken, "It's all hype and theatrics. I've seen it all on TV and it's not for me, thank you very much."

In practice, however, the healing ministry is gentle, simple, and quiet. It is important to remember that Jesus saw each person as whole, healed and at peace with themselves and with God. To achieve that wholeness all we have to do is ask. "If you believe, you will receive whatever you ask in your prayer" (Matthew 21:22).

GIFTS OF THE SPIRIT

"There are different kinds of gifts but the same Spirit; there are different kinds of service but the same Lord; there are different kinds of working, but the same God works all of them in all men. To each one, the manifestation of the Spirit is given for the common good. To one, there is given through the Spirit the message of wisdom, to another, the message of knowledge, by means of the same spirit. To another, faith, by the same Spirit, to another, gifts of healing by that one Spirit, to another miraculous powers, to another prophecy, to another distinguishing between spirits, to another, speaking in different kinds of tongues, and still to another the interpretation of tongues. All these are the work of one and the same Spirit and he gives them to each one just as he determines. The body is a unit though it is made up of many parts and though all its parts are many, they form one body. So it is with Christ."

—1 Corinthians 12:4–12

How generous the Holy Spirit has been to us! Wisdom, knowledge, faith, healing, miraculous powers, prophecy, distinguishing between spirits, speaking in tongues, and the interpretation of tongues—these gifts are given to individuals within a community to use together, to help and guide one another; hence the analogy of one body made up of many parts. Our task is to learn to recognize our gifts and use them for the common good. We may say, "I don't have any special gift." My answer to that is that if you haven't discovered it, you haven't looked hard enough.

Whatever our gifts may be, we can always pray for each other. At certain times in our lives, all of us are all led to pray for others who are suffering. We might not recognize the need to pray, as such. Perhaps we may simply feel an overwhelming sense of compassion, knowing that we want to help. At such times, prayer is the tool we need.

God is the healer. Our job is to allow our lives to become clear channels of God's love, hope, and healing grace. I believe that, like Peter, we need to step out of the boat, to walk in faith and trust that God is working through us for the greater good. Fear of rejection often holds us back, but we need to remain confident in God's will. After all, what is the worst that can happen?

I believe the healing stories told in the Gospels are very real and that the ministry of healing that Jesus demonstrated is based on love, faith, and hope. I hope that this message comes through to everyone who reads these pages.

So the next question is obvious: How can we carry out this ministry in our daily lives? It can seem overwhelming and we might not have the faith in ourselves, but it is important to remember that healing does not come from us; it is from God. There is no pressure on us as individuals if we simply allow God to work through us and go with our inner voice. Take responsibility for your own actions, but know from whence they are sent. With each application, our faith and strength grows, and the next time is filled with even more faith, hope and love.

You may be saying, this is all very well for everyone with special gifts, but I believe that we are all, without exception, given gifts of healing, albeit very different ones. Start slowly, in faith, and be willing to build on your knowledge, through participation in a church or through simply reaching out to a friend in need. Your seed of faith will grow tall and strong and, if it is regularly watered, it will blossom into an exquisite flower.

The fundamental responsibilities in the healing ministry are to listen, love, and pray—pray back what the person has said to you. This is the essence of intercession. Do not give advice (a natural human tendency); do not judge. Become open to God's will. Listen to what is not being said as well as to what is.

How to Pray for Others

"Ask, and it will be given you; search, and you will find; knock, and the door will be opened for you. For everyone who asks receives, and everyone who searches finds, and for everyone who knocks, the door will be opened. Is there anyone among you who, if your child asks for bread, will give a stone? Or if the child asks for a fish, will give a snake? If you then, who are evil, know how to give good gifts to your children, how much more will your Father in heaven give good things to those who ask him!"

—Matthew 7:7–11

Just the fact that you are reading this book shows that you are in touch with God's healing grace and power, but remember that there are many to whom this ministry is foreign, perhaps even suspect, and it is important to remain sensitive to whether the laying on of hands and verbal prayer is appropriate at all. There may be instances when silent prayer for another is the better thing to do. Of course, we may pray for one another at any time and without that friend or stranger even knowing. Many people do this without even thinking about it during, say, a quiet moment at bedtime or first thing in the morning when our thoughts are focused. The simple act of offering prayer for a person in need can be a very moving moment, showing your compassion and love for that person.

This act of offering to pray for someone for the first time can be rather intimidating. That "first step out of the boat" can be very scary. When I first started to pray aloud for others I was very embarrassed and uncomfortable. Negative thoughts haunted me:

"Am I going to say the right thing?"

"Am I going to embarrass myself...even more?"

"You want me to do *what* Lord?"

I would plan out the prayer in my head and then nervously mutter it. I suppose it is rather like riding a bike. At first one is very wobbly and will probably fall more than once. But we pick ourselves up and try it again—crawl, totter, walk, run. The "Holy Boldness" will come, the wonderful holy confidence will flow and then, just as you did once you learned to ride a bike, you will know what to do without even thinking about it. Words will flow like "living water" from your mouth. You may hear yourself saying words that you did not even think of consciously. You may even hear God speaking in your words. I often find myself saying something that surprises me and realize that it was not me, but God working through me. To be able to get out of the way and to let God work through us is a wonderful place to be.

If we are able to pray in our minds for others and indeed for ourselves in quiet, private prayer, then the next step is to practice on someone you love and then to go out in pairs to bring "the Word" to the suffering. Having gotten over the first hurdle of asking for healing and laying hands on someone, begin to pray in silence for the first few times. Then venture forth, pray as a child, pray from the heart, pray from the soul, really mean what you say, let your mind think it and let your mouth speak it, let it flow. Do not be afraid of silence. In fact, I encourage you to let the silence speak; you will be surprised at what you hear.

Norman Vincent Peale encouraged us to pray for complete strangers as well as our friends and acquaintances. He painted a lovely picture of being in an airport and "shooting" prayers to those around us, especially those in distress or with physical handicaps for whom travel is burdensome and stressful.

On one of the early occasions I was asked to pray for someone, I prayed, in my ignorance, from my own strength. It took me awhile to learn how important it is to get out of the way and "allow" God to do the work. We do not have the emotional or physical strength to do it alone—a lesson I learned the hard way.

I was invited to pray for a woman with dystonia. I arrived at her house and found her in tremendous pain. Her head was twisted to the left as far as it would go. Because of the severe twist of her neck, her family had specially arranged two chairs in the living room—one on the right of her husband's chair so she could talk to him, and the other on the left so she could watch television.

I listened intently as she described her history for an hour or so, and then I laid my hands on her neck. Then I prayed with this courageous woman.

But I prayed from my own strength—a dreadful mistake. The next three days were awful. I felt as if my essence had been drained out of me, right from the core of my bone marrow. I had nothing left, nothing at all. I was fully discharged, empty. I almost crawled to the bathroom. This was a very powerful message. I did not listen to God, I did not listen to the words that "I can do all things through Jesus Christ." I got the first part right, "I can do all things." But forgot the second part, "through Jesus Christ." I forgot the importance of the most basic, significant, and indispensable element in the substance of prayer: Jesus. It was a mistake I will never make again, for it is only in Christ and through Christ that we can carry out this ministry. I know now to get out of the way and let God do the work.

One of the main messages of this book is to teach people that everyone is empowered to pray, for themselves and for others. At the beginning of this chapter, I quoted 1 Corinthians, concerning the gifts of the Spirit. By partnering with God, we can all become channels of love and healing. In this regard, I encourage families to pray for and lay hands on their loved ones, relying on their own faith and love. I am reminded of Melissa, a 21-year-old woman who had been in a coma for four years. Both her parents prayed continuously for her, but they did not know about the laying on of hands; their prayer was the quiet, personal, private prayer that most of us are accustomed to.

We went together to meet Melissa at a nursing care facility. Although I have talked time and time again of the power of simple prayer, adding other tools to the toolbox can only increase that power. With Melissa's parents, I was able to give them another tool by demonstrating the laying on of hands. Touch is therapeutic, and I think that in that simple action Melissa's parents felt empowered, as if they had been given permission to do and use what came naturally. As always, I told them to expect a miracle, however small: perhaps she would smile tomorrow and that in itself would be a miracle.

The next day, her father held her head and, looking deeply into her wandering eyes, he prayed. When it came time to leave, he said good-bye in his customary way and walked sadly away. However, he stopped dead in his tracks as he heard a small, muffled but distinct "bye" from the bed behind him. He got more than the smile he had hoped for; this was the first word she had spoken in several years.

THE LAYING ON OF HANDS

"Stretch our your hand to heal and perform miraculous signs and wonders through the name of your holy servant Jesus."

— Acts 4:30

The Bible contains many references to the healing ministry. But how do we, living in another place and another time, participate in that ministry? Where can we get a gentle "holy boldness" to be able to do this?

I believe the answers lie in prayer and the words, "I can do all things through Jesus Christ, who strengthens me, yet it was good of you to share in my troubles" (Philippians 4:13–14). So I urge you to receive the empowerment, the command, to reach out in Jesus' name to pray for others. And how, exactly, do we do this?

The laying on of hands is at once both a grand and a profoundly simple gesture. The first thing to do is to pray, asking God for discernment. Should we pray? What should we pray for?

Then we ask permission of the supplicant: "May I pray for you, may I lay hands on you?" The next concern is where to place our hands. In my opinion, in areas of emotions, memories, and inner healing the hands should be placed lightly on the head. In areas where concerns are focused on reassurance, hands placed on the forehead and the back of the head can be powerful, or even on the temples as a mother might hold a child's head. Do not massage an area. Always be aware of the amount of pressure you exert; some people can get carried away and in their excitement press hard enough to cause discomfort.

We must remain sensitive to all aspects of the person we are touching. For example, a supplicant may be wearing a wig or a hat to cover the side effects of chemotherapy. In the areas of physical prayer request, the hands should be laid on the area of concern, except when that seems obviously inappropriate. For example, in cases of breast or lung cancer the hands may be placed on the shoulder blades or anywhere on the upper back. I cannot overstate the importance of asking permission before any touch is delivered.

While no particular prayer is required, I offer the following as a guide for words that can be used in healing prayer:

> Heavenly Father, Lord Jesus Christ, as we come into your presence we ask that you grace us with the presence of your Holy Spirit as we acknowledge that when two or three are gathered in your name you are in our midst. Lord, we praise you and we glorify your holy name. I ask that my words be your words, that my hands

be your hands and that you work through me for the healing of N._____. [Place your hands on the head or the area of concern.] N._____ I lay my hands on you in the name of God the Father, God the Son and God the Holy Spirit, beseeching you, Lord, to heal this your servant of _____. [Name the illness or concern.] Thank you God, thank you Jesus, thank you Holy Spirit, thank you Holy Trinity. Amen.

RECEIVING THE LAYING ON OF HANDS

Receiving the laying on of hands for the first time can be an unnerving experience. Our worship seldom brings us into physical contact. And our rational, scientific minds may tell us that healing prayer and healing touch is little more than a panacea.

But healing is in fact very simple, just like receiving a gift. And, just as you would open a gift, be open, curious, expectant to something wonderful. Be open, relax, take a deep breath, and expect your healing. Try smiling. You are receiving prayer from someone who cares about you. Allow your faith to be joined with that of the person praying for you. Try visualizing the gift you are asking for—it helps to believe in it before you see it. Be specific in your prayer request to enable the person praying for you to understand your need, for yourself or for others. However, if you prefer to keep your concern confidential, know that God hears your silent request. You can simply say to the person praying with you, "God knows my request."

Receive the grace of God. God does not want you to suffer, he wants you to be well. Reach out your hand now and simply ask, "Lord in your mercy heal me. Lord in your mercy, hear our prayer."

And, finally, give God thanks for the gifts he has given you.

Afterwards

When you have prayed for someone, don't take the concerns with you—leave them with God. Don't try to carry the pain yourself. Make sure that the moment of prayer remains private.

This is a very personal time and it is important to keep it that way by acting as a conduit for the concerns you are sharing, allowing the prayers to flow between God and the supplicant, realizing that these words are sacred and should never be shared in the wrong context. Talking about it to others can be very distressing; confidentiality is vital. We must never tell anyone about another's prayer request.

Finishing the prayer session can be awkward, but need not be so. A particularly effective strategy is to say good-bye before you pray, leaving when you finish your prayer, allowing the supplicant to remain alone in the presence of God. Of course, this is not always the best course of action and here, as elsewhere, we must discern very carefully what God is calling us to do.

CORPORATE PRAYER

"For where two or three are gathered in my name, I am there among them."

—Matthew 18: 20

Corporate prayer, the joining together in community, combining the prayers of the faithful, can be very powerful, adding strength to our prayers. Few moments are as moving as praying for someone in a group; there is a palpable energy that flows from group prayer as each seed of faith is joined together with a common root system. Tears often flow freely and even an unbeliever may feel the faith surrounding him or her like a warm blanket of love. This love and compassion opens up the door of communication between God and our souls.

Jane was in her early 40s and had been suffering from a speech problem for six years. Her voice had become abnormally shrill and high-pitched, causing her much embarrassment in her daily life, especially in her job as church organist. She could no longer talk comfortably, and singing was out of the question. Just as they did with my sister, who suffered from dystonia, doctors diagnosed Jane's ailment as an hysterical condition. She had been in therapy for many years, to no avail.

In her search for an appropriate diagnosis and healing, a friend at her church lent her a copy of my sister's book, *Dancer Off Her Feet*. Ironically, and very shortly after reading this book, Jane herself was diagnosed with dystonia of the throat and was moved to seek healing prayer.

We arranged a special session for corporate prayer and a team, consisting of myself and the pastor and elders of Jane's church. We gathered together at her home to pray for her healing. After I met with Jane the second time, and after she had read my sister's book, the soil was ready for the planting of the seed of healing through corporate prayer.

Jane had been deeply moved by Julie's story of suffering and ultimate healing, but she was so fragile that the balance between fear and hope was as delicate as an eggshell.

The outcome of this group prayer was that Jane was dramatically healed. I would go so far as to say she was cured of dystonia and the last I heard of her, she was working for the telephone company. Thanks be to God!

HEALING TEAMS IN YOUR CHURCH

An important way you can support your pastor or minister in this ministry is (with permission, of course) to create a prayer team within your church. People should be carefully selected for the team. I think it is critical that they are compassionate, loving, considerate, and discreet. The team can participate in monthly healing services; visit the sick in pairs; they can meet regularly on their own for fellowship and encouragement. They should receive ongoing training under the supervision of the clergy to continually create a feeling of empathy and outreach to those in need. If you feel the Spirit move you, I encourage you to approach your minister about this concept of creating another support team for the parish. In many churches, training for such teams is already available through programs such as Stephen Ministry and the Order of Saint Luke that have formal programs and teachings for pastoral care and prayer designed for use at the parish level.

HEALING MEDITATIONS

There are, literally, hundreds of books of meditations on the shelves of bookstores and I encourage you to browse in them for meditations that pertain to your own life and issues. Meditations are very personal and there is absolutely no one-size-fits all. I remember one woman telling me about participating in a meditation group where the people were supposed to envision themselves walking along a river. In her meditation, she kept imagining herself slipping and sliding and tripping on hidden roots. When her meditation moved to a dark, piney forest, she began to find the peace of mind she was seeking.

Please remember to use following meditations as guidelines. If a meditation in this book is helpful, use it. But feel free to adapt it, change it, or find others that work for you. The following meditation is from my sister, Julie Sheldon. In it, she hears the voice of a gentle and loving God.

Rest. Rest in the warmth of my radiance,
my healing warmth,
my healing warmth that restores and heals.
Bring into that radiance the ones who are suffering.

Be gentle. Be gentle.
If they do not yet believe, first they will be touched
by the warmth and the light
and then they will see and know where
the radiance comes from.
I love my lambs. Their suffering hurts me
and I long that they come to me for comfort.
If they seek the comfort elsewhere, quietly and
gently help me to turn them around, to be drawn
back into my radiance.
I will comfort. I will heal. I will restore.
These are my promises for you to believe.
Take them and use them.
Then you will see and believe.
Amen.

There now follow two meditations, one for healing and one for peace. You can have a friend or a loved one read them to you or you can record them on tape and play them back. Take twenty minutes or so, relax, be aware of your breathing, close your eyes and sink into the fabric of your chair, bed or carpet.

The first meditation is adapted from Matthew 9:20:

MEDIATION FOR HEALING

You are in a warm and sunny place *
You are in a crowd of expectant people *
You feel as if something is about to happen * There is an air of anticipation
around you * Further down the street, a
rumble of excited human voices is heard
until around the corner appears a bearded man surrounded by a group of people
in a heated discussion * As he comes

closer, you edge your way to the front of the crowd and as he slowly walks by, you reach out and touch the blue and white tassels on the end of his robe * Raise your hand with your eyes shut and touch those tassels, feel the warmth and heat of God's healing grace enter your arm, shoulder, spine and neck, your head, hips, legs and feet * If you have an area of concern, bring that radiance to that point in your body that is receiving healing prayer * See this man turn, face you, and smile, and hear him say "Your faith has made you well. Go in peace" * Receive your healing and be well * Amen.

The following meditation is designed for a baptism of healing, a release of concerns and a deep inner peace. It is for groups because it can lead to discussion, but it can also be used by an individual. I like to look at this meditation as a twenty-minute vacation I can take at any time.

Our imagination is a God-given gift and in today's fast-paced living we so often use it to build up worries about the future rather than using it to free ourselves from the stresses of every day life. Build on this meditation in your own fashion to give yourself the peace of God that passes all understanding.

MEDITATION FOR PEACE

You are lying in bed, gently being awakened by the warmth of the morning sun shining on your face * Slowly you open your eyes and you observe the walls of a wooden cabin * You slowly arise, putting your feet on the ground and stretching your body like a cat * You stand and move towards the door * Slowly you open the door and are bathed completely in sunlight * The fresh Caribbean scent of sage fills your nostrils and you feel your body slow down and fill with peace * Slowly you walk down a path surrounded by lush green vegetation * This path eventually brings you to a blue lagoon and a white sandy beach * The water is so clear and inviting that you slowly test the temperature with your toes * It is warm, rather like a bath * You enter the water up to your shoulders * It is so clear, so blue, so warm, it envelops you * To your left there is a shaft of sunlight reaching down from the heavens * Move into that light * Focus the light on your area of concern * Pause in that light and feel God heal you in mind, spirit, body and soul * You move out of the water, up the beach, where you find a log * You sit, and with a small stick you write something in the sand * Remember what you wrote * After a while, someone comes and sits next to you * That person asks you what you need and you tell him * Remember who it is and what you asked for * You both stand and walk towards a large chest * You open the lid together and see an empty trunk * Put into that trunk any baggage, any concerns, any fears, any worries * Unload, dump them into the chest, shed your burdens, known and unknown * Close the lid, lock the lock, take the key and with all your might throw it into the sea * Take one of the handles and allow the person who came to sit next to you to help you to carry this heavy chest to the water * Watch as the light breeze pushes it away * Watch it slowly sink into the depths of the ocean * In the distance, you hear a bell and you return to your cabin, to your friends, renewed, refreshed and remade * Amen.

HEALING PRAYERS

Prayer and meditation are extremely personal, even when expressed corporately. There are many different ways to pray. However, I am incorporating a few tangible, practical suggestions. I hope they are helpful to you whether you are a novice just finding the comfort and power of prayer or whether you are already experiencing the joy of a rich prayer life.

As you can see in the following, we can mingle our own prayers with familiar ones from the Prayer Book.

INTO THE SILENCE

Only in silence can you hear the silence speak.
"What will the silence say to me?"
I cannot tell you and, if I tried, that would not be silence. You must go into it for yourself—alone. Yet you will not be alone. There will be you, the adversary, and the Advocate. The spiritual combat will determine whose side you will choose.
A sobering thought?
But you will be supported by the prayers of God's faithful people here on earth, by angels, archangels and the whole company of heaven, and by God.
Go bravely into the silence and listen.

(The Oratory of the Little Way.)

"O God of peace, who hast taught us that
in returning and rest we shall be saved,
in quietness and confidence shall be our
strength: By the might of thy spirit lift us,
we pray thee, to thy presence, where we
may be still and know that thou art God."

(Book of Common Prayer, 832)

There are many ways of praying. When we
embark upon a prayerful journey, a silent prayer or
meditation can be extremely powerful. In our
minds, we pray as simply as we wish, or as specifically as we wish, in whatever way the Spirit
moves us at the time.

I am reminded of a woman I prayed with who
limped in to an evening class that I was presenting
at a doctor's office on healing prayer. I casually
asked her what had happened to her, to which she
replied she had kicked a piece of furniture because
she was angry at her cat. I asked her if her foot was
broken, but she had no idea. She had not consulted
a doctor. I told her a little about the healing ministry and asked her if she was raised in any kind of
faith. It transpired that her parents did not believe
in God and that she had never been inside a house
of worship in her entire life. I asked her point blank
whether she would let me pray for her foot. To my
surprise, she agreed.

The two of us went into another room, where I
was called away for a moment. When I returned I
was more than a little surprised to find that this
woman had removed her shoe and sock as if she
were in a physician's office, which indeed she was.

Of course, there is no need to remove items of clothing in order to be prayed for and we both burst out laughing after I explained this the concept.

She put her shoe and sock back on and I asked her to rest her ankle on my leg. I held her foot and prayed silently, fearing that the words might intimidate her. When I let go of her ankle, she looked me in the eye, stood up, gingerly putting weight on her foot and walked normally around the room. She looked at me in complete astonishment, and I did not need to be told that the pain was gone.

I asked her if she would do something for me in return: this Sunday, would she find a church, any church, and go and thank God for her healing?

Looking back on it, her answer, that one word, "Yes," was the mustard seed of her faith, the seed of faith needed to allow God's healing grace, the "yes" moment I discussed earlier. It was also a reminder to constantly be aware of each individual situation and use the appropriate tool. This was an occasion when the use of silent prayer was right, because words might well have been in the way.

The Lord's Prayer

If words do not come easily to you and silence does not seem appropriate, a familiar prayer such as the Lord's Prayer can be very powerful and one in which the person for whom you are praying can usually participate. I have wonderful memories of praying with people who are barely conscious who have managed to mouth the words to that familiar prayer with me.

I encourage you to revisit the words of the Lord's Prayer and ponder on each line. Because so many of us learned this prayer as children, we tend to rattle it off with barely a thought. Take some time to savor the words and to let them take on a new meaning. Meditating on any single phrase can be a tremendously rewarding experience.

> Our Father, who art in heaven,
>> hallowed be thy name,
>> thy kingdom come,
>> thy will be done,
>>> on earth as it is in heaven.
> Give us this day our daily bread.
> And forgive us our trespasses,
>> as we forgive those
>>> who trespass against us.
> And lead us not into temptation,
>> but deliver us from evil.
> For thine is the kingdom,
>> and the power, and the glory,
>> for ever and ever. Amen

Get to know a more contemporary version, again taking a phrase at a time, and see if this changes the meaning for you.

> Our Father in heaven,
>> hallowed be your Name,
>> your kingdom come,
>> your will be done,
>>> on earth as in heaven.
> Give us today our daily bread.
> Forgive us our sins
>> as we forgive those
>> who sin against us.

> Save us from the time of trial,
>> and deliver us from evil.
> For the kingdom, the power,
>> and the glory are yours,
>> now and for ever. Amen.

Another familiar passage can bring rich reward to the attentive reader. The Twenty-third Psalm is one of the most familiar passages of the Bible, yet its beauty shines through in any translation.

> The Lord is my shepherd,
>> I shall not want.
>
> He makes me lie down in green pastures
>> and leads me beside still waters.
>
> He revives my soul
>> and guides me along right pathways
>> for his Name's sake.
>
> Though I walk through the valley of the
>> shadow of death,
> I shall fear no evil;
>> for you are with me;
>> your rod and your staff, they comfort me.
>
> You spread a table before me in the
>> presence of those who trouble me;
> you have anointed my head with oil,
> and my cup is running over.
>
> Surely your goodness and mercy shall
>> follow me all
>> the days of my life,
> and I will dwell in the house of the
>> Lord for ever.

The words of this psalm are extremely powerful. Take the time to stop and examine each sentence, truly considering its meaning *"The Lord is my Shepherd, I shall not want."* I can put my trust in the Lord, knowing that all my needs will be taken care of.

"He makes me lie down in green pastures and leads me beside still waters." Handing over to the Lord my very existence allows the calm and peace to overflow in me.

"He revives my soul and guides me along right pathways for his Name's sake." Here is a promise of healing, direction and redirection.

"Though I walk through the valley of the shadow of death, I shall fear no evil, for you are with me, your rod and your staff comfort me." Even when you are at your lowest point and though it seems all is lost, the promise that the Lord is with you is paramount.

"You spread a table before me in the presence of those who trouble me. You have anointed my head with oil and my cup is running over." Forgiveness is spoken of here, of how important it is in healing to be able to forgive. Our heads have been anointed with oil and spiritually we are overflowing with love and faith. We can ask God to pour his anointing oil over the rusty hinges and locks of our closed doors, allowing them to swing open and allow the light, warmth, and love of the Holy Spirit to fall afresh on us.

"Surely your goodness and mercy shall follow me all the days of my life, and I will dwell in the

house of the Lord for ever." This promise of positive thoughts are brought alive in this sentence.
Dame Julian of Norwich said that "all shall be well
and all manner of things shall be well," knowing
that I will be in the Lord's house, both now in this
world, and beyond the end of this life as we know
it.

In this world of stress and frantic pace, we
would all be well advised to heed the words of the
Japanese poet, Toki Miyashina, in his translation of
the Twenty-third Psalm:

The Lord is my Pace-setter, I shall not rush;
he makes me stop and rest for quiet intervals,
he provides me with images of stillness,
which restore my serenity;
he leads me in the ways of efficiency through
calmness of mind,
And his guidance is peace.
Even though I have a great many things
to accomplish each day,
I will not fret, for his presence is here;
his timelessness, his all-importance, will
keep me in balance.
He prepares refreshment and renewal in
the midst of my activity
by anointing my mind with his oils of tranquillity,
my cup of joyous energy overflows.
Surely harmony and effectiveness shall be
the fruits of my hours,
for I shall walk, in the pace of my Lord
and dwell in his house forever.

Notice the first line, "The Lord is my pace-set-ter." Some people have pacemakers fitted to their hearts. Here is a thought that the Lord is our pace-maker. God can calm us, focus us, and pull us off the fast track of life into a siding for a rest, where we can recharge our batteries, stop and enjoy the view and step back. This is a blessing that we should pray for at least half an hour a day. Surely, it is at the very height of our busy schedules that we should make the time to pray.

PRAYER IN YOUR POCKET

When we begin praying with and for others, sometimes it can be hard to find the right words. It is then that we can delve in our toolboxes and pull out a prayer that someone else has written. Write down that prayer and keep it in your pocket. Search your own memory or prayer book to find it. Write it down and keep it in your pocket or your handbag, ready to pull out when the need arises. In this way, you will have a tool at your fingertips at a time when words escape you. The two following prayers are from the Book of Common Prayer:

> [N._____], I lay my hands upon you in the Name of our Lord and Savior, Jesus Christ, beseeching him to uphold you and fill you with his grace that you may know the healing power of his love. Amen.

Or:

> [N._____], I lay my hands upon you in the Name of the Father, and of the Son, and of the Holy Spirit, beseeching our

> Lord Jesus Christ to sustain you with his
> presence, to drive away all sickness of
> body and spirit, and to give you that vic-
> tory of life and peace which will enable
> you to serve him both now and forever
> more. Amen.

Of course, a prayer can be tailor-made for the
situation. The following is a prayer from the
Oratory of the Little Way.

> [N._____], I lay my hands on you in
> the Name of our Lord Jesus Christ, ask-
> ing you, Lord, to remove these juvenile,
> delinquent cancer cells that should not
> be in your body, to quietly remove them
> one by one and replace what is taken
> with your peace, your love, and your heal-
> ing grace. Amen.

If you are uncomfortable with this type of formal prayer written by someone else, make up your
own and carry it around in your pocket.

You can also use the "prayer in your pocket" to
bring yourself comfort and peace in times of stress.
Just as mothers say prayers with their children at
bedtime to comfort them and help them to sleep
peacefully, so we can draw on that comfort again
by carrying such a prayer around with us. What a
lovely thought to be able to pat our pocket knowing what it contains.

PRAYING FROM THE HEART

Extemporaneous prayer, to a lot of people, is
terrifying. The thought of touching someone and
speaking from the heart is a bit like diving off the

high board at the swimming pool. After listening to the prayer request, which may or may not be specific, we take the words and pray the history, being as accurate and genuine as possible, speaking in love and empathy from the heart. The transition from silent prayer to praying from the heart is a matter of trust but is really only taking the silent prayer and verbalizing it. The first time this happens and we allow the Holy Spirit to move us in this way is very powerful and joyous. Often, we will begin to speak only to find that these wonderfully centered words, the content of which we are completely unaware, will flow effortlessly from our lips. Of course, the best place to begin in any area of healing is perhaps with a close relative or friend with a simple disorder such as a headache.

LISTENING PRAYER

Surprisingly, listening prayer can be used in personal devotion. We may offer an opening sentence, and then just sit and listen. Although listening prayer can be likened to meditation, it is important to distinguish between the two. We generally think of meditation as musing and contemplation. It often does include listening, but it is not a form of active listening. Though we are constantly asking God to fulfill our needs and the needs of others, it is equally important to listen actively. After all, a conversation with God cannot be only one-way; to be a genuine conversation, both you and God must participate.

For practice, try listening to people before you try listening to God. Try hearing what someone is

really saying and make a point of listening with
your eyes as well as your ears. How often, in
today's society, do we devote ourselves to our own
agendas and take nothing more than a "by your
leave" for someone else's concerns. We do not
even listen to our own spouses and loved ones
because we are so intent on our own thoughts and
issues. We barrel headlong and stubbornly along
with our own thoughts and answers, too busy to
listen to anyone else. How guilty we are of not
really listening to the answer when we ask someone, "How are you?"

Almost invariably the response is: "I'm fine."
But is the person just being polite, knowing you
really don't want to know?

It takes a little courage to look into a person's
eyes and ask, "How are you really?"

It is by learning to truly listen to others that we
are able to learn how to listen to God. It takes time,
infinite patience, and keen inner hearing, but
brings a greater balance to our relationship.

Learning to listen to God can be difficult and
frustrating. Our minds are often overflowing with
practical considerations, and it can be hard to put
them on one side in order to move into that quiet
empty space from which we can listen. Think of
your mind as a radio, receiving whatever signal
happens to be the nearest, the strongest—when it
gets too loud, turn it off. Make it a habit to write
down the practical thoughts as they arise, thereby
shaking them loose of your consciousness.

Ask yourself what it is that God wants us to hear, see or experience. Listening prayer can bring about an awareness of our surroundings so that we can be more attuned to what is going on around us. If we truly listen to God, we will see things that we might otherwise miss completely, for example something as simple and joyous as someone smiling at us in the supermarket will take on a new meaning.

Sometimes, during listening prayer, we are given specific information, the meaning of which only becomes apparent at a later moment. Learning to do this is not easy. As I was learning the technique of listening prayer, I spent twenty minutes a day in silence, listening, not asking for anything. After five days, I had heard nothing specific although I did find a greater awareness of what was going on around me. On the fifth day, I heard quite clearly the words, "right elbow, man, tennis." I wrote them down on a piece of paper and I put it in my pocket. I went to work expecting someone to walk in with their arm in a sling, but no one came. I even called some friends to see how their elbows were, but everyone was just fine.

By three in the afternoon, I had forgotten the whole thing. At four a woman with advanced Lyme disease called, asking me many questions about the ministry of healing. She asked me if God had ever spoken to me directly, at which point I pulled out the piece of paper in my pocket and said "right elbow, man, tennis?" There was silence on the other end of the phone line.

I said "hello?" There was more silence; I said "Hello?" again, in a louder voice.

Finally she spoke. "I don't believe it. When my husband was jogging yesterday he jumped over a fence and broke his right elbow. He's extremely upset because he's a tennis player. Not only that, he suffers from acute tennis elbow." In this case, this word of knowledge became the key to open the door for this woman to seek healing for her own condition.

As in any relationship, communication is key. If we do not listen actively, we cannot hear. The same applies to our relationship with God, and it is only through listening that we will be able to learn from God's wisdom.

We are so accustomed to asking God for something, it may take us some time to adapt and learn to listen.

ACTIP

ACTIP is the acronym of Adoration, Confession, Thanksgiving, Intercession, and Petition. I find the ACTIP prayer very powerful, especially when I am very tired. The words are printed in the form of the Cross:

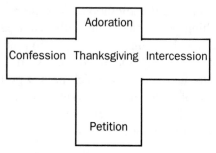

Adoration opens the doors of communication by loving God. In confession we state our sins, known and unknown. In thanksgiving, we thank God for everything in our lives. In intercession, we pray for others; and at the base of the Cross, holding it up, is petition, where we pray for ourselves personally, our own needs and wants.

HEALING PRAYERS FROM THE ORATORY OF THE LITTLE WAY

A PRAYER FOR THOSE WHO LIVE ALONE

I live alone, dear Lord,
Stay by my side,
In all my daily needs
Be thou my guide.
Grant me good health,
For that indeed, I pray,
To carry on my work
From day to day.
Keep pure my mind,
My thought, my every deed,
Let me be kind, unselfish,
In my neighbors' need,
Spare me from fire, from flood,
Malicious tongues,
From thieves, from fear,
And evil ones.
If sickness or accident befall,
Then humbly, Lord, I pray,
Hear, thou, my call,
And when I'm feeling low,
Or in despair,
Lift up my heart
And help me in my prayer.

I live alone, dear Lord,
Yet have no fear,
Because I feel your presence
Ever near.
Amen.

A PRAYER FOR THOSE
WHO HAVE BEEN ABUSED

Dear Lord,
I have memories that need to be healed,
Pain so deep and wounds uncongealed.
Help me in my journey of healing
From those who have given me pain.
Help me with those feelings,
That I may gain
The gain of perfect peace within my mind.
The word "forgive" makes me shudder.
I don't know how.
The word "forgive" makes me utter
And groan with a deep spirit of pain.
Lord, I give you my memories of abuse,
Locked away in my mind,
So private and mine.
Lord Jesus, I know you are kind,
And were present at the time.
Help me now
To release all that pain and suffering.
I release that to you.
You are the healer and you care.
Help me to forgive,
If I dare.
Amen.

A PRAYER FOR THOSE
BEING HEALED OF CANCER

Dear God, I know you are there,
I know you care.
Be with me with this dis-ease
And help me,
Every hour, every minute, and every second.

Lord God, dear Jesus, I humbly add my prayer
To all those who are praying for me.
I add my mustard seed of faith, however small
To those prayers.

Lord, I believe,
Help my unbelief.

Dear Jesus, take those cells in my body
That should not be there,
For I know that you care.

Take those cells,
Those delinquent cells,
And remove them from my body.

I ask that what is taken
Is replaced
With a mighty peace,
The peace of the Lord
That passes all understanding.

Lord, I give you this concern,
And rest in the knowledge
That you love me
And
Are healing me now.
Amen.

PRAYER FOR A SICK CHILD

Lord Jesus, you said:
"Let the little children come to me,
And do not hinder them,
For the kingdom of God belongs to such as these."

It is so hard to watch a child suffer, Lord,
Help me to pray in a powerful way,
To reach this child in your healing grace.

Bless my hands, Lord, that I may
Lay them on this child,
In your name,
For the ministry of healing.

Let me be an instrument of your peace.
Flow through me, Lord.
Let my hands be your hands,
Let my words be your words
So that this child may be healed,
In the name of Jesus Christ.

I give you this concern, Lord,
Fully and with no reservations.
I hand it over with complete
And utter faith
That you are with this child
At this very moment.

Lord, I believe,
Help my unbelief.
Amen.

A PRAYER FOR THOSE
SUFFERING WITH DEPRESSION

Lord God, I ask that you lift
The dark cloud of
Depression
From my being.

I do not own it,
It does not own me,
And I give it all
To you.

I give you that familiar place
That I go to on occasion,
That dark room in my mind.
I ask you, Lord, to shine
Your healing light into
That room to create
A peace and healing grace.

I address those cells
In my brain
That are prone to depression,
And speak your love and positive
Disposition into them.

Shine, Jesus, shine,
Shine your light
Of healing grace
Onto me.
Amen.

WHAT TO EXPECT

Expect a miracle! I think it's important that we believe before we see. God knows our concerns before we do, so expect a miracle as an outcome of prayer. For the wonder is not prayer, but answered prayer, however small the evidence may be. The Bible tells us "to continue in prayer and to watch in the same with thanksgiving" (Colossians 4:2); that is keep praying, keep expecting a miracle, be aware of what is happening and thank God for any such signs. Sometimes, while praying for others, physical manifestations of the Holy Spirit may express themselves. Occasionally hands get hot, some people report a sense of electricity passing from the pray-er to the pray-ee. Some report a deep, inner trembling. Some experience visible trembling of one or both hands. Sometimes nothing is felt but a deep peace. When first beginning in this ministry, we may feel drained after praying with someone, but as we progress, we often become energized.

A Final Word on Thanksgiving

> "We give you thanks, O God, we give you thanks, calling upon your Name and declaring all your wonderful deeds."
>
> —Psalm 75:1

As children we are taught to say thank you to others when they do something for us, and our parents remind us endlessly by asking, "What do you say?" As adults, we still need to express our gratitude, but ideally we become mature enough to know that we must continue to say thank you for gifts, seen and unseen. So it is with God's healing grace that we need to pray our gratitude for healing, before, during and after the gift of healing has been received. As this book nears its completion, I am filled with thanks for the gift of writing, which enables us to portray God's words to others. I hope and pray that it will move you, inspire you and lead you on a journey that brings you closer to God and to your own personal healing and that of others around you.

Lord, I ask that those who read this book
May be called upon to use the gift of healing,
Be open to receive the gift of healing
And to be drawn into your love
As they learn to love, listen and pray.

Thank you God,
Thank you Jesus,
Thank you Holy Spirit,
Thank you Holy Trinity.

Teach us, Lord,
To continue in prayer
And watch in the same with thanksgiving.
Be well in the name of Jesus. God bless you.
Amen.